# HOW TO OPEN AND OPERATE
## A HOME-BASED
## COMMUNICATIONS BUSINESS

"I can only wish this book was available when I was going through the throes of start-up! Not only does it move the reader along nicely through each step and thought process, but it manages to inject a sense of the satisfaction and enjoyment that comes from developing your own business."

—Mary S. O'Connor, founder and principal,
Strategic Communications

*Home-Based Business Series*

# HOW TO OPEN AND OPERATE A HOME-BASED COMMUNICATIONS BUSINESS

by Louann Nagy Werksma

The Globe Pequot Press

Old Saybrook, Connecticut

Cover and text illustrations by Kathy Michalove

**Library of Congress Cataloging-in-Publication Data**

Werksma, Louann Nagy.
  How to open and operate a home-based communications business / by Louann Nagy Werksma. — 1st ed.
     p.    cm. — (Home-based business series)
  Includes bibliographical references and index.
  ISBN 1-56440-631-8
  1. Home-based businesses—Management.  2. New business enterprises—Management.  3. Public relations firms—Management.
4. Advertising agencies—Management.  5. Communications and traffic—Management.  I. Title.  II. Series : How to open and operate a home-based business series.
  HD62.38.W47    1995
  658'.041—dc20                                                95-23999
                                                                      CIP

Manufactured in the United States of America
First Edition/ First Printing

*For Jared, whose birth made me a mother
and a home-based-business owner*

# Contents

# Acknowledgements

First, my sincere gratitude to Mike Urban, vice president and associate publisher of Globe Pequot Press, who gave me the chance to be an author and displayed unlimited patience (even though he couldn't possibly have felt it) as he granted extension after extension.

I offer my thanks as well to:
The clients and colleagues who contributed their time, advice, and ideas, especially Gordon Miller, Rich Nemesi, Tim Breed, Patti Eddington of WordStudio, Mary S. O'Connor of Strategic Communications, and Pamela Patton of Paragraph Writing Services. Also, Calvin Meeusen, C.P.A., and Tom McCarthy of State Farm Insurance for their advice and expertise.

My friend and fellow writer Patricia Mathews Ward, for her thorough and helpful editing.

Other friends and fellow business women who encouraged and sympathized as I stressed and obsessed, especially Jeanne Coppola, Helen Lystra, Jody Sielski, and Amy Wisner. I'm glad I no longer have to answer the question "How's the book coming?"

My friend and mentor, Maggie Dana, who freely shared her bounty of wisdom, experience, and contacts to help me launch Wordwerks in 1986 in Old Saybrook, Connecticut. I cannot even imagine being where I am today without her unstinting generosity and sincere desire to see me succeed.

Most important, Hank Werksma, my best friend and partner in every sense of the word, for always being there for me; and our sons, Jared, Matthew, and Patrick, who make work necessary and life joyful.

# Introduction

"How lucky you are to work at home!"

That's often what I hear when, at a party or other function, I meet someone new and we go through the social dance of exchanging names, occupations, and the ages of our children.

Usually, I nod and smile and agree that I am indeed fortunate to be going on my thirteenth year of earning a living from the same address where I live. And in an occupation—public relations and communications—for which I am trained and well suited. One that I thoroughly enjoy and that doesn't pay badly, either. Unless . . .

Unless it's a day such as the one last January when, during the third weekday in a row that my three sons were all home from school because of a relentless blizzard blanketing the lakeshore towns in West Michigan . . . and when the baby-sitter was at *her* home with pneumonia . . . and when workmen were pounding away at renovations to our 100-year-old Victorian money pit; and I, locked in my office over the garage, fighting with a feckless fax machine that wouldn't send an index for a book that was due at the printer the next day, heard a crash followed by three faint uh-ohs. I abandoned the fax machine and hurried downstairs from my office to discover one of our recently refinished six-panel solid wood doors rent asunder—this because my three sons, when cooped up in the house during a blizzard, think the ideal activity is to chase each other around with sticks until the child being chased flings back a door against the molding and splits it in two. And this was in the part of the house that had already been renovated!

With no time to handle this parenting problem correctly, I ushered the boys back to the television set, promised them an appropriate punishment when I could get around to it, returned to my office with its ringing phone and beeping fax machine, and in my best professional voice fielded a call from a client.

That—and more—all happened before noon.

That evening, my husband phoned from the airport (*he'd*

spent the day at a meeting in Washington, D.C.—with adults). "When you get home, don't even turn off the car engine," I said through clenched teeth. "Just slow down and throw open the door as you pass the house; I'll be waiting to jump in. I've found a baby-sitter and we're going out for drinks and, after about six or seven, possibly, dinner."

There are pros, and then there are cons, of working for yourself, by yourself, in the place where you (and your family) also sleep and eat. In the twelve years I've been at it, I've moved up—and down—from a corner in a den, to a spare bedroom, to an office built for me in a basement, to my current comfortable private office over my garage with its own entrance for clients and a locking door between it and the residential portion of the building. I've graduated from two file cabinets with a Formica board across them and an electronic typewriter charged to my Macy's card to custom-configured, color-coordinated modular office furniture, two computers with modems, a copy machine, a laser printer, a fax machine, a couple of phones, an answering machine, and enough dedicated computer outlets and phone lines to establish a Grand Haven, Michigan, office for NASA.

I'm a pioneer out here on the information superhighway, serving clients from California to Chicago to Connecticut, with suppliers as far away as Alabama, via phone, fax, and Fed Ex. A fellow home-based businessperson says we're "jettisoned out in our pods," orbiting around corporate America, with skills for hire. Skills that are necessary to the corporate world, and that companies often lack owing to "downsizing" of their own in-house public relations, advertising, and corporate communications departments.

Recently compiled statistics show that thirty-two million Americans are now working—either for themselves or an employer—in their homes. By the end of this century, it is predicted, fully half of all Americans will be working from home. Companies that employ home-based workers find that overhead goes down while productivity goes up. Companies that hire the services of home-based businesses find highly skilled professionals who come at their call and work night and day (without time-and-a-half for overtime) to get work out on time and on budget.

Most days, I love being one of that rapidly growing group of people who make a living from an office at home. Today, for example, things are clicking along pretty well. A designer I work with dropped off a proof of a client's newsletter before 9:00 a.m. I checked it at the dining-room table while I drank my coffee and Matthew, my middle child, ate his waffles. While putting away clean laundry, I hired a photographer for a shoot next month from the phone in my bedroom. I got to my office by ten and spoke to one client about an upcoming project, interviewed another solo PR practitioner by phone for this book, and, with the sounds of my children playing (happily, at last) on the swing set in our backyard, I'm writing away.

The ringing of the phone interrupts my concentration and bursts my bubble of home-based-business bliss. The call was from my number one freelance graphic designer, someone who's been designing the majority of my clients' print pieces for more than a year, with news that a proof for another publication will be here by three—and, by the way, he's taking a part-time job at a local newspaper and he won't have as much time to work on my projects as in the past.

Down to the kitchen for coffee and a muffin, and back upstairs to begin flipping through my phone file for names of other freelance graphic designers I can start bringing up to speed on my publications.

Just another day operating a home-based communications business. And yes, I still think I'm lucky to be working from home.

# 1

## Are You Suited to Self-Employment?

### An Exercise to See If You're Ready to Become a Solo Act

My guess is that as a reader of this book you fall into one of four categories.

1. You work for a company and would rather not.
2. You work for a company and face layoff or, to use that enchanting euphemism, "rightsizing." (Ask people who've been "rightsized" out of their jobs just how *right* it feels to them.)
3. You work for a company and want to start a family yet have the flexibility and self-determination parenting often requires. (That was me in 1982. Increasingly, both men and women fall into this category.)
4. You have been out of the work force for either of the reasons in items 2 and 3 and think you might like to start your own home-based communications business.

# Test Your Entrepreneurial Quotient

Whichever of these categories best describes you, it's likely that you're wondering if you have the right stuff to go it alone. If so, you might get a needed boost of self-confidence from a quiz developed by the Northwestern Mutual Life Insurance Company of Milwaukee, Wisconsin.

Titled "What's Your E.Q.?" (for "entrepreneurial quotient"), it's based on research that shows that successful entrepreneurs share common characteristics, such as similar family backgrounds, early experiences, motivations, personality traits and behavior, values, and beliefs.

While this quiz cannot predict your success, it can tell you if you'll have a head start or a handicap with which to work. Entrepreneurial skills can be learned. The quiz is intended to help you see how you compare with others who have been successful entrepreneurs and to help you consider whether you really want to build your own enterprise. Add or subtract your score as you go along.

_____ Significantly high numbers of entrepreneurs are children of first-generation Americans. If your parents immigrated to the United States, score plus 1. If not, score minus 1.

_____ Successful entrepreneurs are not, as a rule, top achievers in school. If you were a top student, subtract 4. If not, add 4.

_____ Entrepreneurs are not especially enthusiastic about participating in group activities in school. If you enjoyed group activities—clubs, team sports, double dates—subtract 1. If not, add 1.

_____ Many entrepreneurs preferred to be alone as children. Could you keep yourself amused for hours when you were younger? Yes? Add 1 point. No? Subtract 1 point.

_____ Those who started enterprises during childhood—lemonade stands, family newspapers, greeting-card sales—or ran for elected office at school can add 2 because enterprise usually can be traced to an early age. If you didn't initiate enterprises, subtract 2.

_____ A lot of entrepreneurs were stubborn as children. If you had to do things your own way and/or learn things the hard way, give yourself 1 point. If not, subtract 1 point.

_____ Caution may involve an unwillingness to take risks, which could be a handicap for someone contemplating a home-based business. Were you cautious as a youngster? Yes, subtract 4. No, add 4.

_____ If you were daring or adventuresome, add 4 more points.

_____ Entrepreneurs often have the faith to pursue different paths despite the opinions of others. If the opinions of others matter a lot to you, subtract 1. If no, add 1.

_____ Being tired of a daily routine often precipitates an entrepreneur's decision to start an enterprise. If changing your daily routine would be an important motivation for starting your own enterprise, add 2. If not, subtract 2.

_____ Yes, you really enjoy your work. But are you willing to work overnight? Yes, add 2. No, subtract 6.

_____ If you are willing to work "as long as it takes" with little or no sleep to finish a job (and your energy stores and family circumstances will allow you to do just that), add 4 more.

_____ When you successfully complete a project, do you immediately look for another? Yes? Add 2 points. No? Subtract 2 points.

_____ Would you be willing to spend your savings to start a business? Yes? Add 2 points. No? Subtract 2 points.

_____ Would you borrow from others? Yes? Add 2 points. No? Subtract 2 points.

_____ If you started a business and it failed, would you start thinking about trying another one? Yes? Add 4 points. No? Subtract 4 points.

_____ Or, if your business should fail, would you immediately start looking for a job with a regular paycheck? If yes, subtract 1 more.

_____ Do you believe being an entrepreneur is "risky"? Yes, subtract 2. No, add 2.

_____ Many entrepreneurs put their long-term and short-term goals in writing. If you do, add 1. If you don't, subtract 1.

\_\_\_\_ Handling cash flow can be critical to success. Do you think you can handle the ebb and flow of cash in a business in a professional manner? If so, add 2. If not, subtract 2.

\_\_\_\_ If you are easily bored, add 2. If not, subtract 2.

\_\_\_\_ Optimism can fuel the drive to press for success in uncharted waters. If you're an optimist, add 2. Pessimist? Subtract 2.

\_\_\_\_ Total

## Scoring

*35 or more:* You have everything going for you. You ought to achieve spectacular entrepreneurial success (barring acts of God or other variables beyond your control).

*15 to 34:* Your background, skills, and talents give you excellent chances for success in your own business. You should go far.

*0 to 14:* You have the ability to thrive in an enterprise of your own, especially if you concentrate on some basic business skills to improve your chances of success.

*-1 to -15:* You don't have a lot of built-in advantages but, like many successful entrepreneurs, you can make up for this with careful planning and by choosing the right business.

*-16 to -43:* Consider carefully before you invest in a business of your own. You may be most productive and your talent may thrive in a more stable environment.

# Test Your Communications Quotient

Here are more questions I created to test your C.Q. (communications quotient). Answer them to determine if you will be successful operating a home-based business that caters to the communications needs of other enterprises.

\_\_\_\_ Are you persuasive? (In other words, do you like to sell?) Yes, add 5 points. No, subtract 10 points.

_____ Are you outgoing, confident, and assertive? Yes, add 5 points. No, subtract 10 points.

_____ Can you handle myriad details and deadlines at the same time without getting stressed out? Yes, add 5 points. No, subtract 10 points.

_____ Do you crave neatness, order, and adherence to preset schedules? Yes, subtract 10 points. No, add 5 points.

_____ Can you put in a full workday and get projects done even when no one is looking over your shoulder or asking for things from you? Yes, add 5 points. No, subtract 10 points.

_____ Do you depend on your earnings for money to live? Yes, add 5 points. No, subtract 10 points.

_____ Are you good at making and maintaining professional connections? (Are you an effective networker?) Yes, add 5 points. No, subtract 10 points.

_____ Are you creative? Can you quickly identify needs that others may not even know they have and come up with a way to meet those needs? Yes, add 10 points. No, subtract 5 points.

_____ Do you have significant public relations, sales, marketing, events planning, fundraising, or other business communications experience, either as a paid professional or a high-level volunteer? Yes, add 5 points. No, subtract 10 points.

_____ Are you used to—and dependent upon—having someone make your copies, type your letters, manage your schedule, and get things fixed for you when they break? If yes, subtract 15 points. If no, add 10 points.

_____ Total

## Scoring

*30 to 60:* Keep reading. The plentiful self-employment opportunities in public relations and business communications await you.
*10 to 29:* Perhaps you need to develop your skills and improve your chances of success by getting more experience in the profession before you strike out on your own, but don't give up on the idea.

*9 to -100:* There are additional interesting home-based careers detailed in the other books in this series. Call or write The Globe Pequot Press for a catalog.

We often see ourselves differently from how others see us. If you'd like an added measure of confidence about your aptitude for entrepreneurial success, give someone else—an objective and trusted colleague, mentor, family member, or friend—a copy of both quizzes and ask that individual to answer the questions as they relate to *you*. Then average the two scores for your final score.

To help you decide if a home-based business is right for you, let's take a look at what you can expect.

# The Pros and Cons of Home-Based Self-Employment

Here are the most important advantages of working for yourself from home.

### Top 10 Advantages of a Home-Based Profession

1. No long commutes; car expenses go way down.
2. You're there to see your kids grow up (and sometimes fall down).
3. You don't have to ask for time off or account for your whereabouts.
4. Clothing expenses are much lower; two or three good "dressed for success" suits or outfits each season are all you need when calling on clients.
5. When you wake up at four in the morning and cannot go back to sleep, you can put in several productive hours and earn a few hundred dollars before the house begins to stir.
6. You derive certain tax advantages from being in business and using space in your home to earn your living.

7. When there's a blizzard outside and your neighbors are scraping off their windshields and preparing to plow through snowbanks, you're heading down the hall or up the stairs to the office in a warm sweater with a cup of coffee in your hand and a smile on your face.
8. You are the master of your own fate, the creator of your own job.
9. When you're in a bad mood, you can screen your calls and keep yourself from alienating the people with whom you work. The only side of you that you ever need show is your sunny side.
10. Sometimes, there are very large checks in your mailbox.

Now, the downside.

## Top 10 Disadvantages of a Home-Based Profession

1. You must arrange and pay for your own health insurance and pension benefits.
2. You have to create every dollar you bring in by finding the clients who need your services and convincing them you're the one for the job.
3. Sometimes, it's a long time between big checks in the mailbox and, by then, you've bought groceries with your credit card.
4. There are certain tax *dis*advantages if you work for yourself at home. Specifically, there's no employer to pick up the other half of your FICA (social security) payments, so you pay approximately 15 percent of your taxable income in self-employment tax, over and above your federal, state, and local employment taxes. If you employ anyone else, you also have the expense and added paperwork of unemployment insurance and worker's compensation payments. If you work by the book (which you should), you have to take time for licenses, regulations, and paperwork . . . and no one pays you for doing this.
5. There's no computer repair department to call when your

hard drive crashes and no supply department where you can go help yourself to paper clips and yellow pads. Nothing gets done unless you do it.

6. The office is always nearby. Unfinished business and unfulfilled deadlines often hang heavily on your mind while you're preparing dinner or playing with the kids.

7. You never have a paid vacation or sick day. When you charge for your time and talent, you don't earn a dollar unless you're physically there producing services.

8. There's no one there to bounce ideas off or to listen to a particularly good piece of promotional copy. It can get lonely.

9. Your friends and family—if you don't train them otherwise—tend to think you're not working and call or drop in right when you're on deadline.

10. When it comes to both work and revenue, it's often feast or famine.

I happen to be one of those home-based business people who enjoy the advantage of a spouse who (so far) earns a living, with benefits, in the corporate work force, so I do not have to set aside some of what I earn to pay for health insurance. Although my income is necessary, my husband's regular paycheck makes it possible for us to sustain the occasional interruptions in my company's cash flow. As we all know, however, this could change at any time. In fact, the only "job security" any of us has is that which comes from confidence in our own skills and a well-maintained network of professional contacts.

# How I Came to Be a Home-Based-Business Owner

I've found myself to be particularly well suited to self-employment. The last of five children by a long shot (my siblings ranged from sixteen to twenty-one years old when I was born), I was raised alone by quiet, middle-aged parents who appreciated books and music. Countless hours spent alone in my room reading as a youngster contributed to my writing skills.

When I was with my peers, however, I liked to organize and lead. Never much of a team player, I was an officer of every club I joined or always found a way to run things. When I began my professional career, it was in smaller, entrepreneurial organizations that needed me to be a self-starter and handle various duties, and I thrived on that. I easily become bored and I get impatient with meetings and the slow pace by which decisions seem to be made in bigger companies.

In 1980 I went to work as a sales coordinator for a smallish (then $6 million in annual sales) manufacturer of disposable hospital products and quickly was promoted to sales support manager for the company's national sales force of seventeen. I thrived on the wide variety of responsibilities and activities, which included daily contact with everyone on the sales force, planning sales meetings, working with customers, coordinating special-order production schedules, designing brochures, creating direct-mail campaigns, streamlining clerical procedures, and buying computer workstations while supervising a staff of five sales coordinators. My workdays often lasted well into the night, but I didn't mind because I loved everything I was doing and my husband was working equally long hours and finishing his college degree at night.

I won't give my former employer a plug here, because I'm still annoyed that, while I was on an eight-week maternity leave in the spring of 1982, the company eliminated my position and moved my sales coordinator staff into the customer service department.

But I have to admit it was the nicest thing that anyone's ever done for me and say thank you very much. During my entire pregnancy, when I had time to take the walks my doctor recommended along the roads of the rural Connecticut town where I lived, I dreamed and prayed and hoped for some kind of work I could do from home while I raised my child. I had filled in between full-time jobs in the past with various freelance assignments, including jobs as a publicist and business manager for a company that conducted writing seminars and as the publicist for a handcrafts school and gallery. As a part-time reporter for a metropolitan daily newspaper on a distant suburban beat, I covered local events and then wrote my articles on a computer terminal at home and sent them via modem to the paper.

I knew I could work from home, but I'd never made a lot of money doing it; and the lure of full-time employment and a regular paycheck had in the past always won out over my desire for independence. But here I was with a new baby, who wasn't sleeping very much at night (or during the day for that matter) and who had completely captivated me. I didn't relish the idea of starting over with the stresses of a new job and company and leaving my infant son in a day-care home for ten to twelve hours a day. Reality, however, loomed large. With my income gone and only partly supplemented by unemployment benefits, we were facing serious financial difficulty. I continued to look for work.

And then my prayers were answered. Nine months after my son was born, and just as my unemployment benefits were ending, I discovered that a publisher of business journals and books had quietly moved into a small office building not far from where I lived. This was unusual because our little house was surrounded by eighty-three acres of big woods, and there were more horses in the town we lived in than there were people. But here it was: a fledgling company that, it turned out, needed a variety of publication production assistance and marketing expertise.

I became a freelance proofreader, then a copyeditor, then a magazine writer and editor; and then I wrote a textbook package, including an instructor manual, for the company—all of which I did from home. But the textbook wasn't selling, so the company convinced me to go to work for it full time as a marketing director for a newly formed educational services division. My son was by then three and entering preschool, and we'd moved to a bigger home in another town (at mid-1980s Connecticut real estate prices); so once again a manager's salary looked very good. I made a one-year commitment to getting the division up and running, and then I hit the road.

During that year I traveled all over the United States, introducing the company's products to customers at trade shows, conventions, and seminars. When I returned to the office, I managed the production of books and audiocasette educational programs. I hired the talent, edited the manuscripts and scripts, and shepherded the products every step of the way. In short, I was responsible for all the revenue and expenses of the division, as well as all the major marketing decisions for its products. I acquired a great deal of extremely valuable experience that year.

But I made a lot of sacrifices, too, and my family made sacrifices on my behalf. In the spring of 1986, my son turned four and I realized I didn't remember much about his being three. All that traveling around the country that had seemed so glamorous when other people were doing it was, in fact, downright unglamorous and tedious to me. I grew weary and discontented through a winter of kissing my son and husband good-bye on Sunday nights and driving through the cold and dark to a crowded, noisy airport and boarding one or two crowded, noisy planes, only to spend a sleepless night in another look-alike hotel room in a city I wasn't going to see much more of than the inside of its taxicabs and convention center.

I learned my lesson once and for all that year. I didn't like the structure, demands, and hours of a corporate job. When my year was up in June 1986, I gave notice that I wasn't renewing for another, even though I had been asked to stay. I trained a replacement and left with a contract for freelance product development work. I dusted off my typewriter in the spare bedroom and went back to writing part time at home.

## Opportunity Rings

But the projects I had counted on weren't forthcoming, and it was evident by August the company, which had been in financial difficulty, was not going to survive. (It went out of business a year later.) One rainy day while my son was napping and I was feeling depressed and not a little desperate I received a telephone call from an employment agency I'd registered with *six years earlier*. I'd never even been sent on an interview with the agency and had completely forgotten about ever going there to look for work. But they had a typesetting job available and a record search revealed that I could type eighty-five words a minute for five minutes with virtually no errors—so would I be interested?

Well. I was not only *not* interested, I was insulted. I told them I was the former marketing director of such and so and the former sales support manager of thus and such and I was in no way interested in their ten-dollars-an-hour typesetting job.

Later that day, I looked in my checkbook and called them back.

Some say that luck is when preparation meets opportunity. I say luck is knowing when an opportunity has disguised itself as something else. On that rainy day in August, I met someone who would turn my life around and put my home-based career on fast forward.

Bear with me. There's a lesson in here and it's one that anyone who wants to survive solo should know about.

## Where There Are Thorns There Might Be Raspberries or Roses

The company, which provided book production services (editing, typesetting, printing, and binding) to many major publishers, happened to be less than a mile from my home. I'd driven past the big yellow building many times on my way to the supermarket and never had any idea that my future mentor was working away inside.

Her name is Maggie Dana, and to this day she is one of my best friends and most trusted colleagues in the home-based-business world. When I called to follow up on the typesetting position, Maggie and I hit it off right away and scheduled an interview. I was honest with Maggie. She hired me even though she knew I was developing my own business and would work only on an interim basis.

Maggie's primary job at the company was as sales representative; but because she was such a good typesetter herself (and a superb teacher) she hired and trained the typesetters. The company provided me with a monster of a machine (called a "bigfoot") that took up the entire surface of my kitchen table. By night, I typeset books and by day I continued to develop my new business, Wordwerks Communications.

Whenever I turned in work I had typeset, I sent along a page or so of notes about errors I had found and corrected in the manuscripts, errors that a succession of copyeditors had overlooked. Maggie took note and invited me to accompany her on the train to New York one day to visit the production editors of several publishing houses. The following week, I had my first book manuscript to copyedit.

Maggie left the printing company two months later and, with partner Jamie Temple (another great friend and colleague), founded Pageworks, a laser typesetting business she and Jamie operate successfully from their respective homes that has served at different times as both client of and supplier to Wordwerks Communications.

I was glad to be done with typesetting and even happier to be a freelance copyeditor. Copyediting led to other, bigger projects with publishers. Eventually, I became a developmental editor of business books. (This is someone publishers hire when a manuscript needs substantial rewriting. ) That in turn led to my ghostwriting books for authors who didn't have the time to write their own manuscripts, but whose names would sell a book.

You might wonder what being a book editor has to do with developing a business communications company. Not much . . . except that

- it provided a steady, predictable stream of revenue from a reliable source (meaning one that always paid its bills).
- I was getting paid to read business books on topics such as launching your own business, telemarketing, writing fundraising letters, creating a business plan, and other helpful advice for start-up businesses, as well as books written for the larger, corporate world—books that gave me insight into the needs of potential clients. (Basically, I got paid to acquire the equivalent of an MBA's worth of knowledge.)
- I developed relationships with people who went on to work in other businesses, many of whom have hired me for completely different kinds of projects and who have referred me to others, so that to this day I'm still earning a living, in a sense, from that endeavor.

The moral of the story: Self-employment is a lot like sour-dough bread. Just as each loaf provides the beginnings of another, one job leads to another.

Opportunities crop up in the most unexpected places. Eventually you learn to discern between great and not-so-great opportunities, but in the beginning I advise that you explore them all.

If I had not changed my mind that rainy August day and called back, my life would be very different today. Probably, I would have gone back into the work force to help pay the bills, and ended up the same way, time and time again: disillusioned and tired of making money for someone else.

My brief, undistinguished association with one company as a typesetter led not only to an editing career and a blossoming business communications firm but, even more important, to a lifelong friendship and business relationship with a terrific individual. Her network of professional associates, through her generosity and sincere willingness to see me succeed, became my network of professional associates.

In 1987 Maggie also referred me to the owner of a growing company that needed someone to write fundraising letters for major nonprofit concerns. For the next three years, while editing books for publishers and doing marketing, PR, and communications work for corporate clients, I also wrote copy for fundraising campaigns that benefited the New York Shakespeare Festival, New York University School of Law, the Wharton School, Yale University, the Jimmy Fund, the People With AIDS Coalition, the Seattle Art Museum, many major hospitals . . . and dozens of other clients. Along the way, I picked up a lot of useful information about nonprofit development—how to raise money effectively—which is a service Wordwerks provides today for *its* nonprofit clients.

If you have worked in this business—or any business—and you've been good about making and maintaining professional connections, you can probably list a dozen people right now who will need the services of a freelance communications specialist. Number one is probably the company you're working for right now.

You might surmise that clients dropped in my lap. In fact, some did. Somedays you work really hard and come up with very little. Other days it rains money. The really fun part of this business is the ring of the phone. You never know what kind of opportunity is on the other end, or down what path it might lead you.

In my experience, finding clients is not hard. Everywhere you look, you see evidence of firms that could benefit from better communications and marketing methods. (So many image problems, so little time.) And you can be just the one they hire to help them improve their image and communicate more effectively.

It's how you conduct business once you have clients that determines your long-term success. As one fellow home-based communications professional—Patti Eddington of WordStudio in Spring Lake, Michigan—said to me, "My professionalism is my best promotional tool."

I've watched many others in my position flounder, give up, and go back to working for others. Since my one brief retreat back to the work force, I've had other offers of employment—some clients just seem to insist on observing you while you work—and each time I've said no, thank you. I'm just too satisfied with this way of work and life to change things right now. And I am more productive and creative without the interruptions of meetings and coworkers who drop by the cubicle to chat.

Some people find they are not suited to self-employment. One friend of mine who was downsized out of a corporation and parlayed his skills and contacts into a successful consulting firm quickly returned to the work force. "I just don't enjoy working by myself," he explained. "I like the stimulation of a big company and lots of people around me."

It's up to you to decide if you agree with my friend . . . or if you're more like me and thirty-two million others who happily serve the needs of corporate America from offices in their homes.

If you've learned enough about home-based self-employment and your aptitude for it in this chapter and you want to give it a try, it's time to get your home-based communications business off and running. In chapter 2 you'll decide what your company will do and who its clients will be.

# 2
# Selecting Your Specialty
### Recognize Your Limitations and Capitalize on Your Strengths

Given what you already know about my company's client list and services, which have varied from copyediting manuscripts for publishers to creating marketing plans for small businesses to fundraising for nonprofits to producing print communications for corporate clients—and a whole lot of other ventures—you might think I'm the last person to advise potential home-based businesses on how to specialize. There have been times in the past twelve years when I've thought I should rename my business "Anything for a Buck, Unlimited."

But then again, perhaps you can learn from my experience. Because today I concentrate on what I do best, what activities and services produce the most revenue in the time I have available to work, and I hire talented people (as subcontractors, not employees) to provide the services at which I do not excel.

This is my "skills inventory" of what I do best:

- Develop rapport with clients and help them uncover their communications needs
- Assess their markets and determine the most cost-effective way to reach them

- Research and write copy for press releases, newsletters, brochures, catalogs, business plans, employee manuals, seminar workbooks, audio and video scripts, and other corporate communications products
- Manage the design, production, and distribution of finished products

Although I work on desktop publishing equipment, I am not a graphic designer. I recognize good design and have a knack for finding good designers and working well with them. My clients appreciate the simplicity of having to deal with only one firm—Wordwerks—for all facets of a project.

I'm skilled at the kind of efficient coordination and careful follow-up necessary to shepherd a product through design, graphic art and photography, type, layout, preproduction, printing, and distributing. I once also developed and maintained client mailing lists and served as a "lettershop" (a business that does the actual folding, stuffing, sorting, and metering of bulk mailings), but I found that not all clients needed these services and that there are other providers who perform them much more efficiently than I do, so I hire this work out today, as well.

I do very little editing for publishers any longer because it does not pay as well as my other ventures. This is a source of regret, however, because editing is something I thoroughly enjoy. It is probably because so many people enjoy it that publishers have been able to keep the fees so low. I still get occasional calls from book production companies asking if I'll take an editing assignment, and if the book itself sounds interesting and the schedule isn't impossible I say yes. Editing is great fill-in work between longer projects, and it is also terrific mental exercise. Except for the cost of red pencils, paper clips, and Post-it notes, there's very little expense involved; and it is a portable task. I've edited manuscripts on planes, in hotel rooms, and on beaches. (I can hear production managers saying, "So that's how the sand got between the pages.")

As my family has grown, the hours I have available to work have diminished; yet every year my business has earned more revenue and my income has steadily increased. That is because I learned to be more productive, and I have developed and promoted my skills to the point that my services are in demand and I have little or no "downtime." (I wish I had more downtime sometimes. You'll find out why when you get to the chapter about organizing and managing your own business.)

# What Is a Communications Company?

Every business and organization on the planet must communicate or collapse. The extent to which businesses communicate and the quality of their communications efforts set the successful apart from the so-so. Under the umbrella of business communications come a great many specialties:

Publicity
Media relations
Community relations
Crisis management
Strategic planning
Employee relations
Productivity improvement programs
Customer service training programs
In-house communication
Customer communication
Media advertising
Direct-mail marketing
Marketing research and analysis
Situation analysis
Corporate identity campaigns (logo and image development)
Annual report preparation
Development/fundraising
Events planning

And there are many more. Each area requires specific professional knowledge, which can be acquired from experience, formal education, personal research, or a combination of all three.

All of these specialties, however, demand one prerequisite. You must be a good communicator, and recognize good communication, to develop programs and projects for your clients.

Nearly anyone can learn how to create a press release in the accepted format or produce a newsletter or a brochure. Or do enough research and ask enough questions to learn the ins and outs of typography and printing processes. One hour spent in a public library can give you a current list of important television, radio, and press contacts.

Not everyone has the intuition and skill to target the customers, understand their needs, fashion services to meet those needs, and find a way to sell them the services. Researching your market is an essential part of business development. The library, the telephone, books, trade journals, your network of personal contacts—all these are the tools you will use to research and develop the right business for you.

Much of what your business becomes will be dictated by business trends and market needs. A willingness to be flexible will help you as you swim with all the other fish in the business sea and decide what color fish you will be.

# Customize Your Business

The exercises that follow are going to seem familiar. You might think they resemble the activities of a job search. That's because they are—with an important difference. For the first time, you won't be writing a resumé tailored to an existing job; you'll be tailoring a job to fit *your* resumé and *your* unique skills and aptitudes. Begin by listing your skills inventory on the accompanying form.

## Skills Inventory

List here, from most to least recent, your job titles, their duration, and the major skills you used in those positions. Include, if applicable, volunteer and civic duties. Photocopy this page if you need additional space.

| *Job Title* | *From* | *To* | *Skills Used/Learned* |
|---|---|---|---|
| 1. _____ | __/__ | __/__ | _____ |
| | | | _____ |
| | | | _____ |
| | | | _____ |
| 2. _____ | __/__ | __/__ | _____ |
| | | | _____ |
| | | | _____ |
| | | | _____ |
| 3. _____ | __/__ | __/__ | _____ |
| | | | _____ |
| | | | _____ |
| | | | _____ |
| 4. _____ | __/__ | __/__ | _____ |
| | | | _____ |
| | | | _____ |
| | | | _____ |
| 5. _____ | __/__ | __/__ | _____ |
| | | | _____ |
| | | | _____ |
| | | | _____ |
| 6. _____ | __/__ | __/__ | _____ |
| | | | _____ |
| | | | _____ |
| | | | _____ |

## What Do You Know—and Like?

Now analyze your list carefully, with highlighter pen in hand. Think about your jobs. When were you happiest? What did you look forward to doing? If you are motivated when performing a job you like, then finding the discipline you need to work alone in your home office won't be a problem. Highlight the skills you enjoy most; then, in the five blanks below, list them from most to least favorite. (If you have more than five, choose only the top five.)

### What I Know (and Like) Best

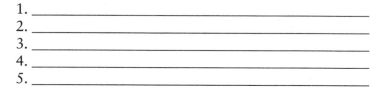

1. _____
2. _____
3. _____
4. _____
5. _____

## What Do You Need to Know?

Are the skills you listed the ones you have used throughout your career? Are they up-to-date? In other words, are they not only the skills you *like* best, but the tasks that you *do* best? If not, and you plan to make a living competing with other professionals who do these things well, determine what you need to do to make yourself commercially successful doing what you like to do best.

Careers are coming that haven't even been dreamed of yet— and you *can* teach old humans new tricks. Desktop publishing is proof. In the 1970s, when working from home was at an all-time low, the personal computer and desktop publishing software were about to be introduced and, almost instantly, blow wide open the world of work. Without these essential tools of my trade, I'd probably still be working for others.

Taking courses isn't the only way to acquire the skills and knowledge you'll need. You can step up your networking efforts by joining professional associations. You should establish a relationship with a strong and willing mentor. Read books and jour-

---

**Desktop Publishing Yields Business Boom for PR Specialist**

Patti Eddington, the owner of WordStudio in Spring Lake, Michigan earned a degree in journalism from Michigan State University and worked as a reporter for three newspapers before joining the public relations staff of a large city hospital. Although she had no background in design up to that point, "that was about the same time that desktop publishing was taking hold," according to Patti, and she discovered she really liked designing as well as writing.

So, with plans to start a home-based business and a family, in that order, Patti took courses in layout and design and became both writer and designer of publications for her clients. One of the publications she writes and designs has won design awards three years in a row from the Michigan Schools Public Relations Association.

"But I know my boundaries," Patti added. "I don't get in over my head." Like Wordwerks, WordStudio subcontracts to other designers and artists if a project calls for special skills.

---

nals on your subject and your target clients' industries. You can take a part-time job in the new area to become more familiar with it.

Think about what you can do to bring yourself up to speed, as fast as possible, on the skills and knowledge you'll need to create your own business. Then fill out the action plan that follows. (The first one is done for you.)

## Education Action Plan

*What I Need to Do*                                    *Deadline*

1. Read *How to Open and Operate
   a Home-Based Communications Business*
   and complete all exercises.                    _____

2. _____    _____

3. _____    _____

4. _____    _____

5. _____    _____

## Whom Do You Know?

Analyze your work likes and dislikes in light of what you think you can sell to client companies. Then use the accompanying form to list all the people you know—your personal and professional contacts—who work for or own a business that can

- give you advice,
- hire your services, or
- supply your business with subcontractor talent.

Include in your list:

- Coworkers
- Firms that supply your employer and the people you know in those firms
- Clients of your employer and the people you work with in those firms
- People you know from industry or trade associations
- People you know from civic or charitable organizations
- Your spouse's personal and professional contacts
- Former coworkers who've gone to work for others or started their own businesses
- Retailers and service businesses you patronize

I am in no way suggesting, if you currently work in a marketing or public relations firm or advertising agency, that you "steal" your current employer's clients. My philosophy has always been "There's enough business out here for everyone." In fact, if you handle your transition from employed to self-employed properly, your employer may become a willing source of clients. Everything you will do as a home-based business, you will do yourself. Your personal and professional ethics will be inextricably linked. The sources of your staying power in your home-based business are your reliability, professionalism, and good name.

I ask you to list all your current professional contacts, including clients of your employer, because every contact is a potential source of future referrals and business—as well as valuable mentor relationships. People change jobs. The universe is in constant motion. A network of contacts, well maintained, is an essential ingredient of home-based business success.

## Find a Mentor

As mentioned earlier, a chance meeting with my friend and mentor Maggie Dana had a lot to do with the early success of my business. A mentor relationship, often touted as the means to success in the corporate world, can be invaluable as you create and build your own business. Find someone who is now successfully working in a communications business and whose advice you will respect. If you cannot think of anyone right off the bat, join your local chapter of the International Association of Business Communicators (IABC), the Public Relations Society of America (PRSA), or Women in Communications, Inc. (their addresses and phone numbers are listed at the end of this book); or attend meetings of local business networks. You'll be meeting future clients and suppliers as well as mentors.

## How Are You Special?

Your combination of education, experiences, aptitude, and motivation are unique. But how will you translate your uniqueness into a specialty that can support you and your dependents? The answer lies not only in what you can do, but in what services are in greatest demand in your marketplace.

## To Whom Will You Sell Your Services?

Based on your assessment of your skills and your list of contacts, identify potential clients. Do not limit yourself to the town in which your home office will be located. If you select your niche carefully and promote your services effectively, your company's influence can extend into the far reaches of the country, perhaps even the world.

For example, let's say you've been producing an employee

## Who I Know

| Name | Title | Company | Address | Phone |
|------|-------|---------|---------|-------|
|      |       |         |         |       |
|      |       |         |         |       |
|      |       |         |         |       |
|      |       |         |         |       |
|      |       |         |         |       |
|      |       |         |         |       |
|      |       |         |         |       |
|      |       |         |         |       |
|      |       |         |         |       |
|      |       |         |         |       |
|      |       |         |         |       |
|      |       |         |         |       |
|      |       |         |         |       |
|      |       |         |         |       |
|      |       |         |         |       |
|      |       |         |         |       |
|      |       |         |         |       |
|      |       |         |         |       |
|      |       |         |         |       |
|      |       |         |         |       |
|      |       |         |         |       |
|      |       |         |         |       |
|      |       |         |         |       |

newsletter for your employer, a manufacturer of medical supplies. You're good at what you do, you enjoy it, and you want to make employee newsletters your specialty. With your credentials and medical manufacturing knowledge, you might explore the following client groups:

- All manufacturing companies within a 50-mile radius of your home
- All medical manufacturers throughout the United States
- Hospitals, nursing homes, and other medical facilities in your state

A trip to the public library to go through telephone books, manufacturer lists, the *Encyclopedia of Associations,* and the American Hospital Association directory will help you compile a lengthy potential client list. You may want to narrow your focus to community hospitals, or to medical manufacturers with sales of $10 million or less (versus sales of more than $10 million), based on your own knowledge and experience within the industry. For example, early research may reveal to you that larger medical manufacturers have adequate coverage in this communications area, but the smaller companies are sorely lacking in regular customer communications. You can further hone and develop this list by comparing it with your own contact list and then begin your marketing efforts at companies where you have connections.

But exactly what is the potential for this market? Your first eager attempts at marketing your services may result in the disappointment of learning that the potential clients you identified don't have a budget for a customer newsletter. Don't give up! You might have the right market, just the wrong service. Listen to what one client company has to say about its communication needs.

## PR + HR = A Winning Combination

"To me, PR is a human resources issue, " says Tim Breed, manager of community relations at Hackley Hospital in Muskegon,

Michigan. "We can develop the best marketing and community relations programs in the world, we can blanket the community with our billboards and ads; but if a customer walks into this hospital and has an encounter with an unhappy worker, then all that time, money, and talent has gone for nothing."

Tim believes the hospital's staff of 1,100 is his "number one customer group" and therefore the community relations and human resources departments must work as partners to educate and motivate those who deal with patients, potential patients, and their families. "People who work here must be informed about what we're doing and must understand how important customer satisfaction is to their—and the hospital's—success." To put the emphasis on customer service, the hospital recently created and filled the position of customer service coordinator.

Such information always sets off my business opportunity sensors. What kinds of programs and projects could support the hospital's efforts? Could we create staff incentive programs to promote customer service and support ongoing community relations? Does the client need a customer satisfaction survey developed and the results tabulated? Before long I've worked up a proposal and set up a meeting.

To succeed on your own, you cannot simply wait to be noticed and called by the client. You have to dream up solutions for problems the clients may not even know they have. Keep your eyes open and your ear to the ground. Use your skills, knowledge, and intuition to create value in your target market.

## Writing Your Marketing Plan

Whatever specialty and target market you choose, your marketing plan should include

- a thoughtful, candid analysis of your own skills
- a description of the types of services and products you will offer
- an assessment of the potential market for your services
- your ideas for promoting your services to your target market
- projected costs of marketing

- an estimate of revenues you expect from your successful marketing efforts

Unfortunately, many home-based businesses start out without a marketing plan because they already have clients and they are too busy working for those initial customers to think about the future. Most of the home-based businesses I know have earned their keep initially through projects supplied by former employers or people with whom they had worked at former clients of their former employers. Mine is one of them. Wordwerks started out in late 1986 and early 1987 with three clients:

a New York publisher
a start-up marketing firm
a Chicago-based international publisher of educational materials for cosmetology schools and hair salons

I've already related how the New York publisher came my way through a chance meeting with someone who became a great friend and source of referrals.

The marketing firm was founded by a man I had worked with at my previous job. His firm targeted hair salons throughout the United States as potential clients for marketing consulting based on client surveys and demographic analysis. My job was to analyze demographic statistics and client surveys and write a marketing analysis and plan for each client business.

The publisher of educational materials for cosmetology schools and hair salons became a client through a contact I made while working for my former employer. Pivot Point International remains Wordwerks' top client, and Gordon Miller, now the company's executive vice president, is an esteemed colleague, a valuable customer, and a cherished friend of almost nine years. (He gets his turn to talk about our relationship in chapter 7.)

So here I was, learning how to use a computer for the first time, analyzing demographic statistics for markets from Red Bank, New Jersey, to Modesto, California, and writing marketing plans for service businesses at the same time I was learning

---

### Creating Value

Mary S. O'Connor had an impressive resumé when, in 1990, she left a public relations firm to found **Strategic Communications** in Old Lyme, Connecticut. A journalist by training, she had spent most of a twenty-year career in leadership roles in some of New England's top advertising and public relations agencies, and for nearly five years, she was vice president of communications for Connecticut Mutual Life Insurance Company.

Although her experiences ranged from corporate strategic planning to speech writing, annual-report writing, and media advertising, Mary preferred the role of strategic thinker and planner and she focused her efforts on clients who would value her expertise and judgment in the areas of corporate positioning and image building, both inside and outside the organization.

Mary believes that the key question all would-be entrepreneurs should ask themselves in the planning phase is "Where can I bring value to my client companies?" She found her answer to this question while planning her own marketing strategy.

"I had a plan in my head, but writing my brochure forced me to define to myself and my potential clients where I could add value to their organizations," she explained. "The challenge of communicating, in a very small space, who you are and what you can do became the basis of my marketing plan."

Later, when Strategic Communications was up and running,

---

to copyedit and spec book manuscripts. And Pivot Point wasted no time putting me to work. Even before I had shipped the first issue of *Focus,* the firm's member-school management newsletter, I was on my way to Chicago to teach a marketing class at its international symposium, and that same summer I wrote *People Skills,* the company's communications textbook for cosmetology students.

I didn't have time to eat, sleep, or breathe, much less plan. I was reacting and responding to needs, taking calls and saying, "Sure, I can do that, " and then hanging up the phone and asking myself, "How am I gonna do that?" So see the box titled "Creating Value" to learn from the experience of someone who

Mary made time to create a formal business plan, which she has followed fairly closely. She also emphasized, however, that for solo practitioners, flexibility to respond to changing customer needs is just as important as following a "golden plan."

To find customers, Mary targeted companies she knew, mainly service firms in industries such as insurance, utilities, and education. She developed a list from her own extensive roster of contacts and supplemented it by researching companies in the New England area.

The number of clients on whose projects she is actively working at any given time averages three, and her fees vary depending on the kind of work she is doing. Like most solo practitioners, she finds that work "comes in waves," and that it is often difficult—while working twelve hours a day, seven days a week on a project for one client—to think ahead and plan for that future date when the current project will be done and something else will be needed to generate revenue. She subcontracts segments of the work to other home-based public relations professionals when necessary, and she alleviates the solitude of self-employment through participation in such activities as the Connecticut Valley Chapter of the Public Relations Society of America and volunteer work with various civic and community nonprofit organizations.

As for a comparison between the corporate world and working for herself, Mary says, "I don't miss the benefits and perks, but I do miss the stimulation of other people."

planned her work and worked her plan when she made the transition from employment to self-employment.

# How Much Will You Charge?

Everyone I know in the home-based-business world agrees that the toughest element of doing business is setting a price. The second toughest task is answering the question "What will this cost?" without ducking or flinching.

But I find that naming a price is getting easier as more and more firms look outside for help with work that once was done by inside staff. Home-based businesses tend to have lower overhead and charge less than agencies with leased offices, which makes them very competitive in many areas.

After twelve years, I'm finally comfortable with fee discussions and have developed a fee schedule that I believe is fair to me and my clients. I charge my highest hourly rate for onetime projects or regular projects of fewer than ten hours per month. Similarly, there's a premium charged for "drop-everything-and-do-this-now" client requests.

My rate for larger projects is lower because I believe that economies of scale arise from longer-term projects. Clients who buy blocks of my time per month on a continuing basis (such as a real estate company that calls on me for marketing advice and advertising copy and design services an average of two hours per week) help me to manage my time and even out my cash flow, and I reward that loyalty and trust with my best fees.

Similarly, regular, contracted work that provides predictable income also qualifies for lower rates. I produce periodicals on a contract basis, with prices negotiated annually. My suppliers (graphic designers and printers) know what they will be paid, and that saves them from having to cost-estimate each issue. My client can budget communication expenses. And I can bill a project when it begins, rather than wait until after it has been shipped and all my suppliers' invoices are in. That leads to improved cash flow and preserves my good trade credit.

I recommend that you follow these three simple steps for setting a price:

1. Determine what other firms offering similar services are charging
2. Determine what clients are willing to pay
3. Determine what you need to earn

## Determine What Others Are Charging

You can easily find out what others charge by making telephone calls to firms listed in the yellow pages. Not many home-based businesses that I know have yellow-page listings, so you may have to dig a little deeper to talk to these professionals. Many join their local chambers of commerce or other associations, and I'm sure you know of several friends or former colleagues who are now plying their trade from home. Attend meetings of your local chapter of the PRSA or IABC and get to know the members. Be prepared for price to be a touchy subject with some.

## Determine What Clients Are Willing to Pay

Work your network to discover what companies pay for outside services like those you have decided to provide. Don't be shy. You may find some potential clients while doing this portion of your marketing plan research.

A client who hired me to develop and produce a community relations program told me when I quoted my hourly rate and my estimated monthly invoice, "I'm very comfortable with that. Any more and I would have a hard time justifying your outside services."

In my geographic area, businesses similar to mine charge from $25 to $75 per hour. My rate falls near the middle of this scale; and because my rates are reasonable, the client and I can work comfortably together to develop a working relationship and a publication that speaks to its audience and accomplishes its purpose. If I were to come in at the top level, no matter how experienced I am and how skilled an interviewer and writer I may be, I know I would be judged by a different set of standards. Any errors or missteps on my part would be scrutinized under a brighter light. Whenever I was working on-site, people would be looking at their watches (just as they do in the presence of lawyers and others who charge an arm and a leg for their time).

I know many who do work similar to mine who charge more than I do. I'm always busy. They're not.

## Determine What You Need to Earn

Whatever you do, don't take your present salary, divide your weekly income by forty, and use the result as the hourly rate you'll charge. If you plan to work your business forty hours per week, at best about 75 percent of those hours will be devoted to billable work (the remainder being devoted to development, marketing, and management), and approximately two-thirds of your revenue will be net profit after overhead expenses and before taxes. If you need to purchase health insurance and fund a pension, your "take home" pay will be even further reduced.

So, if you charge $50 an hour and take in $1,500 per week, your taxable income after overhead expenses will be approximately $1,000 per week, or $50,000 per year, for a fifty-week year. That's optimum. There will be downtime. You will get sick. Projects you think are coming in at a certain time might be delayed a couple weeks because the executives at the client companies with whom you're working will not have your company's cash flow needs uppermost on their priority list.

Your overhead costs will vary depending on the kind of equipment you will need and how you will pay for it. If you're going to borrow money or lease equipment, you'll have higher overhead than if you pay for it with a nest egg or severance pay.

Factor in these overhead expenses:

- Loan payments or lease fees, if any
- Telephone
- Stationery and office supplies
- Postage and shipping
- Software
- Computer repair and maintenance
- Cost of upgrading or replacing equipment
- Promotional expenses
- Business insurance (a necessity)
- Travel expenses
- Client entertainment and "thank-you-for-the-referral" gifts
- Bank fees
- Publications and subscriptions
- Licenses and fees
- Electricity and heat for your office
- Expenses for business use of your automobile

Let's say you project to be able to bill 125 hours per month initially (approximately 30 hours per week). Considering that you'll need to spend at least 10 hours per week on developing and marketing your new businesses, and 5 to 10 additional hours on other nonbillable management tasks, 30 billable hours is an optimistic—but still realistic—goal for someone who can spend 45 to 50 hours per week at work. If your overhead expenses amount to $2,500 a month, then your overhead is $20 per hour. If you charge $60 per hour, you will earn $40 after expenses and before taxes. That amounts to $1,200 per week of taxable income.

The ins and outs of financing and start-up costs are the subject of the next chapter, and I'll go into them in more depth there. You need to have an idea of what the competition charges and what the market will bear, however, for your marketing plan, which you should outline, here and now, on the form titled "Marketing Plan: First Draft."

That's just a beginning. By the end of this book, your plan will be fleshed out with fee schedules, revenue projections, and promotion campaigns. For now, however, you've made a strong start. You've begun to give thoughtful consideration to where you've been, what you've learned, and where you can go from here.

Now on to everyone's favorite subject: finance. It's the next step in creating your business plan.

## Marketing Plan: First Draft

Name of business:

Name of owner:

Owner's background, experience, and accomplishments:

Description of services and products:

Target clients and industries:

Differential advantage (how I will add value to my customers' organizations):

Marketing and promotion plans:

Hourly rate and project fees:

# 3
# A Fail-Safe Start-up
## Projecting and Planning for a Profitable Business

While need and greed can be good motivators, I find it's easier to mind the store when you aren't under the stress of more outgo than income. By taking the time to put your personal finances in order and plan carefully for your business's financial needs, you'll start on the right financial footing and your business will have a better chance to succeed. That will in turn allow you to be more selective about your work and more creative while you're doing it. Besides, like bankers, clients can smell desperation. If you don't act as though you really need the money, they're more likely to give you work—at the fees you set—than if they think they can capitalize on your own lack of capital.

Ideally, the experts recommend that you begin your venture with enough capital to cover your business start-up costs, as well as overhead and living expenses for six months. That's the ideal. I can name many successful home-based-business operators who got their enterprises off the ground on far less. I am one of them.

You must assess your own situation and be honest with yourself about how much risk you're willing to take and how many sacrifices you're willing to make. If you have the advantage of strong skills and good contacts, you may have the ability to generate cash quickly. Use the worksheets in this chapter to calculate your business-capital requirements. The information you provide in them will be plugged in to your start-up business plan.

# How Much Do You Need to Survive?

If you've always managed your own personal finances well, you may not need to concentrate on this section of the chapter. I've known Ivy League MBAs, however, who were responsible for corporate millions and yet never balanced a checkbook or had any concept of their own living expenses. Here's my advice to anyone about to become newly self-employed.

1. Get a good sense of your personal expenses and how much income you and your family need to survive.

2. Determine what portion of those expenses will be covered by other income (such as the paycheck of your spouse, severance pay, unemployment benefits, and savings) and explore ways to increase that income.

3. Cut as many unnecessary expenses as possible and prepare to operate your business—and your life, if necessary—on a "lean and mean" basis until you're safely under way.

4. Take care of credit needs before quitting your job. Most banks won't lend to loan applicants who are self-employed until they have two years of income tax returns to show. If you need to refinance your house, buy or lease a car, or set up a line of credit to help finance business start-up, do it while you're still employed by someone else.

## 1. Understand Your Personal Budget Needs

Use the "Personal Budget Worksheet" and guidelines that follow to determine your own personal budget. Remember to figure into your monthly expenses such items as home and auto insurance that you pay quarterly or annually. If you're not the one who writes the checks and makes the purchases in your household, be sure to sit down with the one who does and determine your monthly income needs as precisely as possible. If you don't know what you spend on any of the listed items, look back through checkbook registers and charge card statements to get an accurate idea.

Remember to include expenses that might currently be paid by your employer, such as health insurance premiums and automobile expenses.

Once you've completed the worksheet, let's see what can be done to reduce the "income needed" figure to give your business a little breathing room.

## 2. Increase Income from Other Sources

If you have a working spouse, does he or she have the ability to work overtime or generate income from additional projects? If your spouse has not, until now, worked outside the home, can he or she find part- or full-time work for six months to a year while you get your business up and running? Can teenage children pitch in with part-time work to pay for their own clothes and entertainment?

Working spouses may not need as much federal and state income tax withheld from their paychecks now. If your income will be significantly reduced while you start your business, even temporarily, then your taxable income for the year probably will be lower than in the past. Project your joint income for the year, figure the taxes, and subtract what has already been withheld from both your paychecks so far to determine what should be withheld for the remainder of the year. Once your own income picks up again, reevaluate and, if necessary, reestablish the previous level of withholding.

## 3. Cut Back on Spending

We all let expenditures get out of control from time to time. If you've been living the two-income, too-busy-to-cook-and-clean, married-with-children lifestyle, you probably can rein in spend-

## Personal Budget Worksheet

| Item | Amount per Month |
|------|------------------|
| **Savings and investments (paid out)** | _____ |
| **Shelter** | |
| House payment or rent, including property taxes and monthly association dues | _____ |
| Second mortgage, if any | _____ |
| Home equity line of credit payments, if any | _____ |
| Homeowner's/renter's insurance | _____ |
| Heat and electricity | _____ |
| Telephone | _____ |
| Cable TV | _____ |
| Home maintenance and repair | _____ |
| Home improvement and decor | _____ |
| **Transportation** | |
| Car payment #1 | |
| Car payment #2 | _____ |
| Auto insurance | _____ |
| License and registration | _____ |
| Personal property taxes | _____ |
| Gasoline and oil | _____ |
| Parking fees | _____ |
| Public transportation costs | _____ |
| **Family necessities** | |
| Food and household supplies | _____ |
| Life insurance premiums | _____ |
| Medical/dental (including premiums) | _____ |
| Personal care (barber/beauty, etc.) | _____ |
| Child care | _____ |
| Housekeeper | _____ |
| School tuition, books, and fees | _____ |
| Clothing, tailoring, and dry cleaning | _____ |
| Children's lessons and sports fees | _____ |
| Gifts (birthday, Christmas, other) | _____ |

**Debt**
    Other installment debt             _____
    Credit card balances/minimum monthly payments

_____    _____

_____    _____

_____    _____

_____    _____

**Entertainment/recreation/leisure**
    Dining out                           _____
    Theater/art/sporting events        _____
    Travel                              _____
    Club (health/country/tennis) dues and fees   _____
    Boat dockage/storage/fuel and maintenance   _____
    Vacation home expenses            _____
    Books, magazines, newspapers, music    _____
    Hobbies                            _____

**Other (list)**

_____    _____

_____    _____

_____    _____

_____    _____

**Total monthly outgo (now)**           _____

**Less income from other sources:**

Spouse take-home pay or business profit    _____

Alimony/child support payments          _____

Income from investments/other            _____

Unemployment compensation/severance pay   _____

**Total Monthly Income Needed**          _____

ing. If you have high credit card balances and other consumer debts, do what you can to clear these up and vow to buy only what you can afford from here on out.

One caution I offer from my own experience: If you have small children, don't begin cutting in the categories of child care and housekeeping. So many people assume that because they are home they can work and take care of the children. It just is not so. You cannot develop a business and pay adequate attention to the needs of small children. Older children are a different story. With the right preparation, they can learn to be helpful (and quiet) while you're working.

The same idea goes for housekeeping. If a clean and neat house is important to you, and you know you'll procrastinate getting to your office while you straighten up, consider this: Housekeepers charge from $8 to $15 per hour. You will bill your clients considerably more. Which is a more profitable use of your time?

As for other things on the list that might be deemed luxuries—health club memberships, country club fees, the boat—weigh each potential cut carefully. If you honestly think the country club or marina will be a rich source of potential clients, then perhaps you'd be wise to maintain them. I'll leave it up to you and your accountant to determine the tax-deductibility of such expenses.

Entertaining clients, however, has never been—for me or anyone else I know working from home—a major expense. I've yet to meet a client who expected to be wined and dined by a solo practitioner. In this era of budget cutbacks and downsizing, most clients appreciate the home-based business's ability to deliver quality services quickly and at reasonable prices. My business entertainment expenses average about $100 per month.

Certain expenses of working away from home will be minimized or eliminated: gas, oil, and wear and tear on a commuter vehicle; parking; expensive lunches; clothing, tailoring, and dry cleaning; dinners out when you don't have time to cook; and similar items.

## 4. Refinance and Consolidate Debt

Before you leave your current job, explore the possibility of refinancing and consolidating your debt to achieve a more favorable interest rate and/or lower monthly payments, or both. A low-interest, short-term second mortgage (ten years or less) could help you get out from under high consumer credit payments, give you extra money for business start-up costs, and offer the benefit of tax-deductible interest. Most self-employed business people I know bought equipment and set aside working capital by taking out loans secured by their homes. They arranged the financing while they were still employed.

Keeping a minimum of six months' living expenses and business overhead expenses in a savings or money market account is a good idea. Therefore,

1. Determine a bottom-line monthly personal spending budget.
2. Add 10 percent for unforeseen and unplanned expenses.
3. Subtract from that figure projected income from all other sources except your new business revenues.
4. Multiply that figure times six and enter the result below and in the blank on line 1 of the "Recap Worksheet" on page 58.

Six months' living expenses          $_____

# Start-up Costs:
# Furnishings and Equipment

Start-up costs vary from one home-based business to the next, but it's safe to assume that your expenses will be lower than they are for a company that leases space elsewhere. Most likely, you will meet with clients in their offices, so your environment need not be plush. Your desk chair should be comfortable, however, and your work area should provide good light, insulation from noise and activity in the rest of the house, adequate working surfaces, and storage. It should, if at all possible, be a dedicated space.

### Recommended Start-up Equipment

- Furniture: a desk, a good chair, a worktable, file cabinets, bookshelves, good lighting
- Telephone with a minimum of two lines or phone mailboxes
- Answering machine
- Fax machine (on a dedicated line)
- Computer with modem and laser printer
- Software applications: word processing, desktop publishing, file management, project management, mailing list, mail merge, bookkeeping and invoicing, spreadsheet, translation, and communications (for your modem)
- Copy machine (optional)
- Office supplies: the usual
- Lots of coffee

You can spend as much as $16,000 on this list or as little as $4,500. My recommendation is that you economize in every way possible. When you're rolling in dough you can go out and buy it all over again. For now, don't put that kind of pressure on yourself. Here are my suggestions.

## Office Furniture ($500 to $2,000)

Avoid standard office equipment dealers. They are geared to the environments—and budgets—of big companies. Good second-hand office furniture is available at resale shops and by scouring the classifieds. Reasonable prices are also available at office superstores and warehouse buying clubs. Adjustable metal shelves are inexpensive and will someday make the transition nicely to garage or basement. An eight-foot folding table can be stored flat and put up only when you're working on a big project that requires a large work surface. You can find used versions of these for $50 to $100.

I've been through several generations of office equipment

and furniture. Today my office contains modular office furniture from a store that specializes in it. It's durable, attractive, reasonably priced, and expandable. The store's designer visited my office, drew a plan, and helped me select pieces that would best utilize my space. (There was no charge for her design fees.) A desk and chair, two large bookcases, two worktables, a rolling file cabinet, and a lateral file all together cost me less than $2,000.

I purchased four track-lighting sections, with three cannister lights each, for just over $100 at a warehouse store. Our house is not centrally air conditioned, so a window air conditioner was essential for smooth operation of the laser printer on muggy days and because the equipment generates a great deal of heat.

## Telephone(s), Answering Machine, and Fax Machine ($500 to $1,500)

I lump these items together because they are your communications equipment and you are a communications company. When you are not available to answer your phone personally, your line should be answered electronically or by a service. (I prefer electronically. I find the quality of help at answering services inconsistent and the messages they take inscrutable. Although the attitude of "I hate those machines" still prevails in certain quarters, most clients are perfectly comfortable leaving a voice message and prefer it to having to speak slowly and spell their names for an answering service employee who doesn't know you or your business.)

In many areas, local telephone companies offer services that give you the appearance of a big, busy office with only a touch-tone telephone. For service fees as low as $7.00 per month, you can have one or more voice mailboxes that permit you to avoid putting a client on hold while you take another call (prices vary from area to area; check with your local telephone service company). Instead of interrupting you, new callers will hear a programmed greeting and be given the option of leaving a message. The voice mailboxes take the place of an answering machine when you are not there to answer. The best benefit of all is that these services are now available for home lines, saving home-based businesses the expense of installing a business line.

What about business lines? Do you need one? Yes, if potential customers are going to be looking you up in the yellow pages. If not, then save the cost and make sure you get your name and number in the hands of as many prospective clients as possible.

I recommend that you get a speaker phone so that you can keep your hands free to work while listening to on-hold music. Inexpensive telephone headsets also help you work while you talk. If you can afford it, a cordless radio phone on an extension jack will allow you needed mobility. (Anyone who has ever experienced the frustration of hearing a delivery person pounding on the door at the same time a client is on the telephone will understand the importance of a mobile phone.)

Install a dedicated office line (not an extension of your home phone) and, if possible, a second line for your fax machine. Do it before you publish your phone numbers. I bought a fax–telephone–answering machine combination, thinking I could do it all with one line, and quickly became frustrated with it. The fax is now on a dedicated line, and that number is listed on my stationery and business cards.

Some home-based businesses get along fine without fax machines by using fax modems that allow them to send to and receive from other computers and fax machines. The only drawback, in most cases, is that they have to be home with their computer on when someone wants to fax them something.

Shop around for telephone equipment at the superstores. Good fax machines can be had for $300 (be sure to get a paper cutter), phones and answering machines for $100 each or less. Plan to replace your phones every two years or so. They don't make them like they used to. Furthermore, as your business expands, so will your telephone equipment and service needs.

I also find a cellular car phone very helpful. As a mother of three soccer-playing, baseball-playing, friend-visiting boys, I spend a lot of time in the car. Available everywhere in my area for $50 plus hookup fees, portable or "bag" phones make it easy to make and return calls while on the run. My monthly bills average about $25, which I believe is well worth it.

If you're going to be out of the office a great deal, you might want a pager. Particularly in the start-up phase of your business, when you are awaiting responses to proposals you've drafted, a pager will allow you to respond more readily to potential business opportunities.

## Computer, Peripherals, and Laser Printer ($3,000 to $10,000)

Don't expect a Macintosh-versus-DOS analysis from me. It's been done, in a lot of other places, a lot better than I could ever do it. The general wisdom I keep hearing over and over again (leading me to give it credence simply owing to repetition) is that DOS is better for everything but graphics. When it comes to graphics capability, Macintosh has always been and still is way out in front. Every graphic designer I know owns a Mac. The entire discussion is expected to become moot in the near future, when both companies plan to introduce compatible systems.

I started out working on an IBM PC clone. I didn't have a choice. A client needed me to work on a system like his; he bought the equipment, installed the software, and set it up in my office, and my first $2,000 in billings to his firm paid for it. I bought an inexpensive dot matrix, near-letter-quality tractor-feed printer to go with it, and that was what I used for six years.

Two years ago I bought a used Mac for $500 and a new laser printer for $2,000 because all my designers were working on Macintosh and complaining that my DOS disks weren't translating clearly. The new computer gathered dust for six months while I gathered my courage to tackle a new skill. I finally hired someone to come in and teach me how to use it (total cost $50). I hated it at first. I now love it. I guess you can teach old workers new tricks.

The best advice I ever read on the computer debate is: Decide what software you're going to use and buy the hardware to support it. I add another line: You can learn to use anything. Don't get stuck in analysis paralysis. Make a decision and get on with it. The most important factor as far as I'm concerned is service and support. When my hard drive crashes (it has, and yours will), I want it up and running again fast. If you can find a computer guru who can come when you call, pay him (or her) well. Good computer support is golden.

A computer consultant can also help you develop a plan for upgrading your equipment as you outgrow and "use up" your current computer capacity. The person I consult knows what to buy and where to get it at the best price. His expertise is well worth his fee in terms of time dollars, because he saves me from having to do all the research and running around myself.

According to Walter S. Mossberg, who writes a personal-technology column in the *Wall Street Journal,* someone looking for an all-purpose system to run basic business applications should be seeking a reputable name brand that offers adequate power and good upgradability. Here's some advice from the annual buyer's guide to personal computers that ran in Mossberg's column of September 1, 1994.

First, software applications like word processors and even games are demanding more and more machine to run adequately. Second, PC operating systems, the underlying programs that control a computer, are due for fundamental revisions in 1995. Both Microsoft's new operating system for IBM-compatibles, code-named Chicago, and Apple's new Macintosh operating system, code-named Copland, will require more muscular machines than those typical today. And third, the explosion in multimedia software and in sophisticated, on-line systems puts heavy new demands on hardware.

The good news is that the heftier machine outlined below won't cost you any more than a lesser PC I recommended a couple years ago, because of the constant decline in hardware prices.

*Memory and Disk Storage:* Nothing is more important to a satisfying computer experience than having enough memory (RAM) and hard-disk storage capacity. These factors matter more than small differences in the main processor chip or the computer's brand name. An extra $300 or $400 invested here will pay huge dividends.

Do not buy a PC with less than 8 megabytes (8MB) of memory. If the model you like has only four megabytes of memory, pay extra on the spot to have it expanded to eight megabytes, or add memory chips yourself. Adding four megabytes of memory should cost around $200.

Your hard disk should be at least 300 megabytes in size; 500 megabytes would be better. It's much cheaper to buy extra hard-disk capacity at purchase time than it is later; often another 100 megabytes can be had for $50 or $75. (On a Mac, you might get away with 250 megabytes of hard disk, because Mac programs tend to take up less room.)

*Central Processing Unit (CPU):* This is the main brain of the computer. On an IBM-compatible, I prefer at least a 486 chip running at a speed of 66 MHz (megahertz). On a Mac, you want at least a 68040 chip running at 33 MHz. The top-of-the-line CPU chips are Pentium chips on IBM compatibles and PowerPC chips on Macs. They are so new that few soft ware programs take full advantage of them, and the chips are quirky in some situations. Most good computers now can be upgraded with these speed-demon chips later, though the up-graded machines won't likely be as fast as a Pentium or Pow-erPC model built from the ground up.

*Video:* Get a monitor with "dot-pitch" rating of 0.28 mm or less—a smaller number means a sharper image. Make sure the computer's internal video system has at least one megabyte of VRAM, which is special video memory that makes the screen display faster, and that it can display 65,000 colors or more on the screen, which makes for more realistic images. On a PC, make sure it can handle a resolution of "800 x 600" or better and is "local bus video."

*Sound:* Macs come with good sound. Make sure an IBM-compatible has a built-in sound system that is compatible with the popular Sound Blaster card, and that it comes with stereo speakers.

*CD-ROM Drive:* Even if you don't care about multimedia software, get a CD-ROM drive. You'll need it, because all kinds of software will soon be distributed mainly on CD-ROM. Make sure the drive is rated at "double-speed," with an access time of 350 milliseconds or less (less is faster).

*Modem:* Another essential, especially if you ever hope to ride the information highway. Make sure it has the ability to both send and receive faxes, and that it can send data at a speed of 14,400 bits per second (BPS) or higher. Stay away from the new 28,800 BPS models unless they meet a standard called V.34 or can be upgraded cheaply and easily to that standard. A good model in that latter category is the Sportster from U.S. Robotics.

*Expandability:* Make sure your computer can be upgraded to the next-level CPU chip, has at least one free slot for add-on circuitry inside and can accept at least 32 megabytes of memory.

*Brand Names:* Unless you are a techie, don't buy a superstore's unknown house brand, or a no-name computer from your brother-in-law. . . . Stick with established names that offer good warranties and service plans, like Compaq, Apple, IBM, AST, and Dell. Gateway 2000 and Packard Bell are generally OK, but I consider their quality and customer service to be a bit below that of the first five brands.

Finally, whatever you do, don't let yourself get flustered by some fast-talking salesperson. Stick to your guns on the key features [outlined here].

(Reprinted by permission of the Wall Street Journal, © 1994 Dow Jones & Company, Inc. All Rights Reserved Worldwide.)

If you think you'll need to travel frequently to client locations, consider a laptop, or notebook, computer. By using electronic mail (e-mail), you can send and receive correspondence and documents to and from clients and suppliers, which is a great advantage when you are on the road. You will also have access to on-line research wherever you go.

A modem is also useful when you're writing and someone else is formatting the text and providing graphics. It saves a trip across town or the time and expense of express-mailing a disk. A modem is also great for on-line research and professional development. One on-line service, CompuServe, offers helpful resources for the home-based communications professional (these are described in chapter 5). In addition to CompuServe, other services available include Prodigy, America Online, and local providers of Internet access.

As for your printer, I like laser printers but many people swear that ink jet or bubble jet printers are just as good even though they cost less. As with any computer purchase, make your decision based on your application. Will you be producing camera-ready art and copy? Will you be printing and binding seminar materials? If not, and the output your clients will see will be mostly letters and proposals, you can afford to spend less. Another avenue to explore is service bureaus. These are companies that invest in high-priced, high-powered equipment. They can take your disk and output your files to high-resolution paper plates or film. Many offer scanning capability, color copiers, and a wide array of other services that you may need from time to time.

Don't invest in high-priced printers, scanners, or other equipment you really don't need in the beginning. Ask your computer consultant or local computer retailer for the names of service bureaus and other businesses in your area that have the equipment and provide services for a fee.

One final note: I recommend you purchase a "power surge protector" for your computer equipment. This will keep your system from inadvertently being damaged by high- or low-voltage variations on your electric lines. Your computer dealer or electric utility representative can help you with power quality issues.

## Software ($300 to $1,000)

Once again, here's a list of home-office business basics:

- Word processing, such as Microsoft Word (which I use) and WordPerfect
- Desktop publishing, such as PageMaker and Quark XPress
- Mail list management
- Mail merge
- File management
- Project/time management
- Accounting/bookkeeping (Quicken, QuickBooks, M.Y.O.B.)
- Spreadsheet (Lotus, Excel)

Depending on the computer deal you negotiate, some of your start-up software could be included as part of your hardware package price. Subscribe to *Home Office Computing* magazine (see the bibliography for details) and while waiting for your first issue head over to the library and read back issues of it and other computer support publications. You'll find all the analyses of various kinds of software you could ever want and more than you could ever have time to read. Talk to everyone you know who uses computers at home and to the computer support people in your employer company, if you're still working there or have stayed in touch.

Whatever you do, don't take too long or talk too much. The number one objective is to get up and running. If you make a mistake, just correct it. We're only talking about $50 or $100 per software package. If you don't think you need it right now, don't buy it yet. You'll have enough on your plate without getting bogged down in software installations and manuals. In chapter 4, "Getting Organized," I'll review the available accounting software to help you streamline business financial management.

## Copy Machine (Optional!—up to $1,000)

I got along without a copier for years, but I've always lived near commercial copy centers. You won't catch me standing at a copy machine duplicating lengthy manuscripts or manuals when businesses such as Kinko's and Mailboxes Etc. have sprung up on every street corner and offer support services for reasonable fees (all of which are billed to clients). Since acquiring a $600 Canon copier, however, I have found it to be useful, particularly in making copies of faxed proof so it can be marked up and faxed back. Once again, the rule is: If you don't absolutely need it, don't buy it. Yet.

## Office Supplies ($200 to $500)

I have always maintained an account at a local office-supply retailer. My current supplier is just blocks from my home office (whereas all the superstores are 20 to 30 miles away), so doing business with this outlet is convenient, and the store will even deliver when I'm in a pinch. Prices are fairly competitive with superstores, I don't have to buy huge quantities at a time, and if they don't have something they can get it in a day or two. My favorite feature is being able to run in whenever I need something, grab it, and write one check at the end of the month. (Paying your bills on time helps your business develop trade credit.)

I don't think I have to tell you what office supplies you need and why you'll need them, but just to make it easy on you when you're shopping, I've included a checklist you can photocopy and take with you.

## Office Supplies Shopping List

- [ ] laser printer paper (white)
- [ ] fax paper
- [ ] Rolodex and extra Rolodex cards
- [ ] file folders
- [ ] labels for file folders
- [ ] hanging files, tabs, and indexes
- [ ] stapler and staples
- [ ] tape dispenser and transparent tape
- [ ] glue sticks
- [ ] lined pads
- [ ] Post-it notes
- [ ] paper clips (several sizes)
- [ ] 9" x 12" manila or white envelopes
- [ ] computer disks (lots)
- [ ] computer disk holder
- [ ] computer keyboard brush/cleaner
- [ ] computer and printer dust covers
- [ ] pens and pencils
- [ ] highlighters
- [ ] electric pencil sharpener
- [ ] desk light
- [ ] scissors
- [ ] art supplies (if doing your own layout and presentations)
- [ ] other  _____
         _____
         _____

Let's review your equipment and supplies needs and costs.

| | | |
|---|---|---|
| Office furniture | $500 | to $2,000 |
| Telephone(s), answering machine, and fax machine | $500 | to $1,500 |
| Computer, peripherals, and laser printer | $3,000 | to $10,000 |
| Software: | $300 | to $1,000 |
| Copy machine (optional) | $0 | to $1,000 |
| Office supplies | $200 | to $500 |
| **Total equipment and supplies costs** | **$4,500** | **to $16,000** |

Enter your own expense projections for equipment and supplies in the worksheet here and put your total in the blank on line 2 of the "Recap Worksheet" on page 58.

### Start-up Equipment and Supplies Costs Worksheet

| | |
|---|---|
| Office furniture | $_____ |
| Telephone(s), answering machine, and fax machine | $_____ |
| Computer, peripherals, and laser printer | $_____ |
| Software | $_____ |
| Copy machine (optional) | $_____ |
| Office supplies | $_____ |
| **Total start-up equipment and supplies costs** | $_____ |

# Start-up Costs:
# Marketing and Promotion

This category includes the costs of developing your logo, designing your business card and letterhead, and printing an adequate supply of stationery, envelopes, labels, and business cards. A capabilities brochure is also essential. Marketing and promotion programs are discussed in more detail in chapter 6.

Each time I've needed stationery and business cards designed and printed, I've traded my marketing and copywriting services with designers and printers and paid nothing. I helped one designer write a direct-mail piece and develop a direct-mail campaign. She in turn designed the logo I use today and prepared camera-ready layouts for letterhead, envelopes, and labels. Ditto for the printing. I wrote my printer's capability brochure; my printer printed my stationery.

As for capability brochures, you can go for the really slick and expensive kind or you can spend a lot less and still present your desired image. One way to do the latter is by using attractive, full-color brochure formats available from direct-mail companies such as Paper Direct (listed in the Appendix). Choose from an extensive variety of colors and styles. Write your copy, design the piece on your computer using inexpensive software templates available from the paper manufacturer, and run it through your laser printer—as many or as few as you need.

Even if you don't take advantage of trade arrangements as I did, your initial expenses for design and printing should be lower than most because of your own expertise and contacts. Plan to spend a significant initial amount on postage and telephone, however, as you get the word out about what you're doing and follow up, follow up, follow up.

Adding it all together, a fair estimate for initial marketing and promotion expenses is $1,000 to $5,000. Enter your own expense projections for start-up marketing and promotion here and in the blank on line 3 of the "Recap Worksheet" on page 58.

### Start-up Marketing and Promotion Costs Worksheet

| | |
|---|---|
| Logo design and development: | $_____ |
| Stationery and envelopes | $_____ |
| Capabilities brochure | $_____ |
| Business cards | $_____ |
| Postage and telephone | $_____ |
| Other | $_____ |
| **Total start-up marketing and promotion costs** | $_____ |

# Calculating Projected Overhead

You've seen here that start-up expenses for equipment and supplies can range from $4,500 to $16,000 and that marketing expenses increase that figure by another $1,000 to $5,000, for a total of $5,500 to $21,000. Let's work with an amount in the middle: $13,000.

Now add to this figure six months' of business overhead. Projections for this are based on individual variables. For example, if you're financing start-up costs with a business loan, your business overhead expenses will include debt repayment. If you're purchasing needed equipment and supplies from personal savings, then your overhead expenses will be much lower.

My office overhead expenses in 1993, for my part-time business, averaged $1,000 per month, exclusive of automobile expenses. My business has never carried a debt. My number one expense each month was telephone ($180) followed closely by advertising/promotional expense ($120), office supplies ($100), research materials and publications ($75), and postage/shipping ($50).

Using the "Business Cash Flow Projections Worksheet," list your projected business income less overhead expenses. Multiply your own projection for monthly overhead (expenses) times six months and enter that figure on page 58 in the blank on line 4 of the "Recap Worksheet."

Now, complete the "Recap Worksheet" by totaling the bottom-line results you've plugged in from all four worksheets.

# Financing Your Start-up

I've already mentioned several creative ways I helped finance my business needs. I exchanged services with a client for my computer equipment. I traded services with suppliers to get my stationery and other marketing materials designed and printed. I charged a typewriter to a department store charge card. I

# Business Cash Flow Projections Worksheet

Projected monthly income      $ _____

Cost of goods sold
- Printing      $ _____
- Typesetting      $ _____
- Art and Illustration      $ _____
- Photography      $ _____
- Other      $ _____

Total cost of goods sold      $ _____

Gross Profit (projected monthly
income less total cost of goods sold)      $ _____

Expenses (overhead)
- Office supplies      $ _____
- Telephone      $ _____
- Postage, shipping      $ _____
- Publications      $ _____
- On-line services      $ _____
- Bank fees      $ _____
- Utilities (heat, elec.)      $ _____
- Debt service      $ _____
- Promotional costs      $ _____
- Casual labor      $ _____
- Cleaning      $ _____
- Maintenance      $ _____
- Travel      $ _____
- Entertainment      $ _____
- Professional dues      $ _____
- Business insurance      $ _____
- Accounting, legal      $ _____
- Other (list)

     _____      $ _____

     _____      $ _____

     _____      $ _____

Total expenses (overhead)      $ _____

Net profit/income (gross profit
less total expenses      $ _____

*Note:* Accountants define "cash flow" as "net profit plus depreciation." No line item for depreciation (on business equipment and the business portion of an automobile) is included here because that is a deduction that benefits you at tax reporting time but does not represent actual dollars subtracted from your bottom line. In this worksheet, therefore, "net profit" and "cash flow" are one and the same thing. You would, however, be wise to set aside an amount equal to your equipment depreciation figure each month for eventual replacement of worn and outdated equipment. Talk to your accountant or financial adviser.

### Recap Worksheet

| | |
|---|---|
| Monthly personal expenses times six months | $ _____ |
| Start-up costs: equipment and supplies | $ _____ |
| Start-up costs: marketing and promotion | $ _____ |
| Projected monthly business overhead expense times six months: | $ _____ |
| **Total needed** | $ _____ |

worked as a typesetter at my kitchen table at night to bring in extra money. If you know you can generate revenue from your skills and contacts, there are many ways to unlock the cash you need to get started.

## Real Estate

Most home-based-business operators I know financed their start-ups by borrowing against their homes while they were still employed in-house. This approach offers the advantages of tax deductibility of interest, lower interest rates, and lower monthly payments than would result from an unsecured loan or—perish the thought—a credit card cash advance.

What if, however, you don't have equity to borrow against? What if you don't own real estate at all? Or perhaps you do, but you don't feel comfortable encumbering the roof over your family's head. Everyone should consider the downside potential of borrowing against a primary residence. If your business doesn't get off the ground and you remain without income for an extended period, you might have to sell your home and move. Worse still, you might face foreclosure. Can you live with that possibility?

If not, what sensible alternatives exist?

## Severance Pay

With all the downsizing, rightsizing, and just plain old-fashioned layoffs happening in corporate America, there are plenty of people receiving lump-sum payments of from six weeks' to several years' income. The problem I've seen, however, is that most of those people don't even think about working for themselves until they've already been out of work for six months or more, and by then the severance pay is all used up.

If you are about to become unemployed, I recommend that you not wait too long before you set your sights on self-employment. Consider that it takes an unemployed manager or other professional an average of 1½ years to find a similar job in the United States today. Meanwhile, the ranks of the self-employed are swelling by the thousands each month. If you've read this far, chances are you're more than a little interested in starting your own home-based business. Get started now, while you still have cash on hand. She who hesitates is broke.

## Retirement Savings Plans

This category includes pretax money you've invested through 401(k) and 403(b) plans at your former place of employment as well as the proceeds from lump-sum payouts of vested pension and profit-sharing plans.

Before you cash in your 401(k), be sure you're aware of the ramifications. The most important consideration, as I see it, is that tax penalties and withholding will take about 50 cents of every dollar you have saved. Here's how it works on an account worth $50,000, assuming all funds were invested on a pretax basis.

| | |
|---|---|
| Value of 401(k) account | $50,000 |
| Less 10% penalty for using funds before age 55 | −5,000 |
| Less federal tax (maximum 28%) | −14,000 |
| Less FICA (7.65%) | −3,825 |
| Less state income tax (4% on average) | −2,000 |
| Yours to spend | $25,175 |

I would consider this revenue source only as a last resort. If you are young and relatively carefree, you most likely have time to rebuild your account before you retire. But if you're thirty-five or older, have a family, and this is your only retirement savings, try to manage without spending your last dime. On those really dark days that are sure to come, when you've lost a big account or failed to win a client you were sure would come through, you'll have the solace of knowing that there's still a cushion to fall back on.

## Other Investments

Any other investments—stocks, corporate bonds, U.S. savings bonds, stamp or coin collections, jewelry, artwork, antiques, classic automobiles, the boat, a vacation house—are fair game. After all, you're merely transferring wealth, temporarily. You're transforming an investment in some other enterprise or inanimate object to an investment in your skills and potential. The returns could be far greater than anything you'll ever get from the stock market.

## Equipment Rental and Leasing

If you just cannot raise all the cash you'll need to get started, consider renting or leasing equipment at first. Many computer and office supply dealers offer this option, and some businesses specialize in it. A caution: it's usually quite expensive, so I recommend it only as a short-term solution.

Think creatively. It's your business to be creative! Do you know anyone in business whose computer equipment sits unused, perhaps in the evening? Could you arrange to "rent" time at that office after hours? If your personal circumstances (and energy reserves) permit such flexibility, you could telephone and visit clients by day and complete projects by night until you have sufficient earnings to purchase your own equipment.

## Borrowing from Other Sources

I've mentioned briefly some of the other forms of credit you can employ to raise cash for your start-up. These include

- personal installment loans
- credit card cash advances
- borrowing from family and friends
- advances from venture capital firms
- business installment loans

Personal, unsecured installment loans and credit card cash advances, while they carry a high price tag, may work for you if you know you'll have fees coming in soon and you'll be able to repay the debt ahead of schedule. Be careful. High-priced credit has been the ruin of many promising start-ups.

There may be friends and family members who are willing to help you get started. Private sources of capital don't appear on your credit report, so they don't limit your future borrowing power. I recommend that you formalize any transaction with a friend or relative by drawing up and signing a note and specifying an interest rate and repayment schedule.

Service businesses run by solo practitioners rarely find financing through venture capital firms, but they might under certain circumstances. Venture capitalists normally seek value beyond the skills of an individual, such as would be found in patents, licenses, trademarks, and other elements associated with manufacturing. In exchange for their investment, venture capital firms usually insist on owning a percentage of a business and having oversight of its operations.

Which brings us back to business, or commercial, credit. While it's not the most common form of financing used by home-based businesses, it is still a viable possibility. It could be advantageous for your business to develop a commercial-credit relationship with a bank or other financial institution in your community. As you repay the loan on schedule, you build a foundation for future financing assistance as your business grows and develops.

Be prepared to promise whatever business assets you have, such as equipment and fixtures, as collateral for the loan, as well as to guarantee the loan personally. Then, if you default on the loan and the lending institution secures a judgment against you, it can place a lien on any property in your name—including real estate you own jointly with someone else. It can attach any wages you earn in the future. Unless a judge grants you relief in bankruptcy proceedings, you cannot just walk away from a business debt you have personally guaranteed, even if you dissolve the business.

# Your Start-up Business Plan: An Overview

In order to be successful in securing a business loan, you will need a carefully prepared business plan that outlines for the lending institution who you are, what your skills and experience are, and what plans you have made to assure your success. While you know that you can make it on your own, your banker knows that 80 percent of all small businesses fail within three years. Bankers read a great many business plans and listen to a great many enthusiastic, would-be business owners. They also foreclose on a lot of property and sell off untold dollars worth of business assets.

To get a banker to say yes, you must have more than a dream and a belief in yourself. You must have a plan that clearly explains your capabilities, business structure, and source of projected revenues. In clear, outline form—with facts to back you up, not just assumptions—the plan must tell the banker

- who you are
- what you know
- who you know
- what you plan to do with your background and experience
- the nature and extent of the market for your business
- how much you expect to charge for your services
- what you can realistically earn

A business plan can be broken into five main sections.

1. Executive Summary
2. Resumés of Owners
3. Business Structure/Form of Organization
4. Financial Statements
5. Marketing Plan

While I introduce and describe all the components of the business plan here, you will need to complete the remaining chapters of this book to have enough information to write a strong plan. Section 3 ("Business Structure/Form of Organization") cannot be completed until you've read chapter 4.

You can, however, complete the financial section (section 4). In fact, most of what you need for that section will be at your fingertips if you've been completing the worksheets in this chapter as you have been reading.

## 1. Executive Summary

The first page read by a lending institution, the "Executive Summary" is the last part of your plan you will write. In succinct, clear language, it sums up you, your business plan, and gives the reader a good reason to want to read further. It's your "hook."

## 2. Resumés of Owners

The second section of your plan states who you are in recognizable resumé form. Update your resumé to highlight the career achievements that support your business plan and your request for financing. Limit it to two pages. All partners in the business or, if the business is incorporated, officers in the corporation, should include resumés in the plan.

## 3. Business Structure/Form of Organization

Here you explain your decisions about the legal form of organization your business will take. Your choices are a sole proprietorship, a partnership, a Subchapter S corporation, and a corporation. These four options will be explained in chapter 4. As an appendix to your plan, you can include copies of legal filings and articles of incorporation.

## 4. Financial Statements

*Personal Financial Statement:* If your business will take the form of a sole proprietorship or a partnership, then the assets of the owner(s) will be considered fair game by a lender if there is a default on the loan. Corporate status doesn't necessarily protect your personal assets. Lenders require the owners of many start-up corporations to guarantee the loan personally with real estate or other assets. The personal financial statement of every "principal" of the business—owners, partners, or officers of a corporation—must be included.

A personal financial statement is simple to compile, and a sample form is provided. Construct your statement to fit your personal circumstances. List (and describe) all assets on the left-hand page and all liabilities on the right-hand one. Subtract liabilities from assets to arrive at your net worth.

Other financial statements a lender will look for in this section of your start-up business plan are listed below.

*Personal Income Statement:* This outlines the owner's personal living expenses less other sources of income. Plug in the "Personal Budget Worksheet" from pages 40–41.)

*Business Start-up Expenses:* Plug in the Worksheet "Start-up Equipment and Supplies Costs" (page 54) and the "Start-up Marketing and Promotion Costs Worksheet" (page 55) here.

*Business Cash Flow Projections:* The lender is going to want to see cash flow projections for at least six months, preferably a year. Plug in the "Business Cash Flow Projections Worksheet" (page 57) here. In your actual plan, it will be helpful to include a six-month or one-year spreadsheet, showing income figures increasing each month.

*Total Start-up Capital Being Sought:* Plug in your "Recap Worksheet" (page 58) here and rename it "Start-up Capital Needs."

## 5. Marketing Plan

As a marketing and communications expert, you would do well to be at your creative (albeit realistic) best here. Describe the services and products you propose to market, summarize the research you've done showing market potential, and explain how you will reach your audience and convince them to hire your business. You got a good head start with your start-up marketing plan in chapter 2. I'll discuss creative marketing and promotion at greater length in chapter 6. Till then, every time an idea strikes you, write it down!

We're rolling. In order to get your business plan completed and your business launched, however, we're going to have to pause for a chapter on organizational issues. Bothersome as they may be, little details such as business structure, insurance, zoning regulations, business licenses, sales tax laws, and the like can become vicious beasts that bite you in the behind if you don't address them up front.

## Personal Financial Statement

| Assets | Value |
|---|---|

Real estate: appraised value (list address, description)

1. _____ $_____
2. _____ $_____

Automobiles, boats, recreational vehicles (year, model, description)

1. _____ $_____
2. _____ $_____
3. _____ $_____

Savings and checking account balances (account numbers, name of institution)

1. _____ $_____
2. _____ $_____
3. _____ $_____
4. _____ $_____

Stocks, bonds, and other securities (list each holding and number of shares)

1. _____ $_____
2. _____ $_____
3. _____ $_____
4. _____ $_____

401(k) and 403(b) accounts; other personal investment pensions in which you are 100% vested (list name and address of holding company)

1. _____ $_____
2. _____ $_____
3. _____ $_____

Antiques, art, jewelry, furs, collections

1. _____ $_____
2. _____ $_____
3. _____ $_____
4. _____ $_____

Other personal property
(household furnishings) $_____

Other assets (specify)

_____ $_____

**Total Assets** $_____

# Personal Financial Statement (continued)

**Liabilities**                                    **Balance Owed**

(For all types of indebtedness, list name and address of creditor)

Mortgages
1. _____ $_____
2. _____ $_____

Home equity lines of credit
1. _____ $_____
2. _____ $_____

Charge cards
1. _____ $_____
2. _____ $_____
3. _____ $_____
4. _____ $_____
5. _____ $_____
6. _____ $_____

Auto and other installment loans
1. _____ $_____
2. _____ $_____

Promissory notes made to individuals
1. _____ $_____
2. _____ $_____

Margin account balances with brokerage firms
1. _____ $_____
2. _____ $_____

Other liabilities (specify)
_____ $_____

**Total Liabilities**                              $_____

**Net Worth (total assest minus total liabilities**   $_____

# 4

# Getting Organized
### Make the Right Management
### Decisions Up Front

The myriad details of business adminstration are not, I admit, my strong suit. I much prefer the actual work of a communications company to the management of one.

From the beginning, my approach to business management has been fairly simple. I operate as a "sole proprietorship," reporting my income on Schedule C attached to my federal and state tax returns. I consistently have from four to six active clients at any given time, and I send about three or four invoices a month, deposit the checks the following month, and pay my bills at the beginning of each month. After setting aside a portion of my receipts for tax obligations and my IRA, the remainder gets swallowed up by the family budget. So far, I've not experienced either a receivables or payables problem. I've developed my own simple systems for record keeping and tax reporting, organizing my work, managing my time, and maximizing my productivity.

My way of doing business may not be the best way for you, however. Remember, for the time being I'm happy with a part-time business that allows me to have time for my family, volunteer work, and friends.

I can see a day coming, however, when I'll have the time and desire to expand, take on more work, perhaps hire employees. In the past two years I've seen a steady increase in business, and I've had to refer work to other home-based communications professionals and share projects and fees with them. The well-worn axiom "Standing still is going backwards" reverberates through my head. We live in a dynamic universe. I won't be able to enjoy the luxury of part-time work forever. Besides, there's so much interesting work out there to be done. So, onward and upward!

For a business to grow and be healthy, it must be well managed and thoughtfully planned. I, therefore, approached the writing of this chapter as someone who needed to know the information as much as any of my readers would, and I researched the topics thoroughly. I've gleaned what I believe to be the best advice from experts on the topics of legal form of organization, bookkeeping, tax reporting, zoning, business licenses, and the like. Where appropriate, I've added advice of my own, derived from my personal experiences and the mistakes that taught me well.

# Legal Forms of Organization

Most business in the United States is conducted under one of three forms of organization:

1. Sole proprietorship
2. Partnership
3. Corporation

Of these three, only the sole proprietorship is simple to explain and offers no variations. Partnerships and corporations come in a variety of colors and flavors: general partnerships, limited partnerships, Subchapter S corporations, limited-liability corporations (LLCs), professional corporations, and so on.

## Sole Proprietorships

Nearly 80 percent of all small businesses are operated as sole proprietorships. You become a sole proprietorship by saying you are one. In the case of a partnership or corporation, there are legal documents (and, of course, usually legal fees) involved in creating it.

As a sole proprietor, your business net profit, or income, is your personal income as well. You estimate and pay state and federal income tax and self-employment tax on your net profit (revenue less out-of-pocket expenses, depreciation, and home office deduction) on a quarterly basis. Your business income tax return is a Schedule C ("Profit or Loss from Business or Profession") attached to Form 1040 of your federal income tax return. A similar schedule is provided by states that collect income tax.

Your social security number is the identifying number for your business, unless you also pay employees. In that case, you apply for and receive a federal employer identification number (EIN), which identifies you for tax reporting purposes.

As a sole proprietor, however, your business cannot last beyond your lifetime. You are personally liable for the debts and obligations of your business. If your business is sued and a judgment is secured against it, the plaintiff can attach any assets you own individually or with another to satisfy that judgment. (In other words, the house, the car, everything but the kids could be sold at auction.) As a sole proprietor, you'll need to evaluate your potential for liability and purchase insurance to protect your assets.

## Partnerships

Although sole proprietorship is by far the most common form of organization for small businesses, many home-based business owners opt to work with a partner. There are advantages: someone to share the work and worry; someone whose talents dovetail nicely with yours, who is strong where you're weak and vice versa; someone to mind the store when you go away.

From a legal and paperwork standpoint, a partnership is

only a little more complex than a sole proprietorship and far simpler than a corporation. While partnerships file informational tax returns, they do not pay income taxes. The net income of the business is taxed as personal income according to the share each partner receives.

If you are considering entering into a partnership, you should have your legal adviser draw up a partnership agreement that stipulates, among other things:

- the amount of ownership interest of each partner (will it be a 50-50 split or will one partner hold a controlling interest?)
- what will happen to the partnership in event of the death of one partner
- how one partner can "buy out" the other

A word to the wise: Partnerships break up at an even greater rate than do marriages. Many friends who go into partnership together emerge from the experience as enemies. Early on in my home-based career, I turned down an offer to become a partner in a new marketing firm. The firm grew and eventually bought a printing company. Did I err? I don't think so. The partner with the controlling interest was a high-risk individual who saddled the partnership with so much debt that it eventually went out of business, and those who invested in the enterprise or loaned money to it went unpaid.

I have great relationships with others in this business, and we "partner" on projects all the time. It's sort of like a date versus a marriage. When you're just "dating" you're on your best behavior. When you sign that contract—be it marriage or a business partnership—the stakes get much higher.

I know home-based partnerships that are growing and thriving after many years. My friend and mentor Maggie Dana formed Pageworks, Ltd., with Jamie Temple (another friend and colleague) in 1986. Jamie and Maggie had been coworkers and friends before going into business together. They will both agree that it hasn't always been easy. But their partnership has survived, among other things, Maggie's cancer, the death of Jamie's father and birth of her son, and a temporary separation of the two partners. Maggie moved to Alabama in 1994 to be near her grandchildren, and the partnership, friendship, and business all persevered. It can be done. It just takes very special people to be partners—in business and in life.

## Corporations

Corporations offer the benefit of creating an entity separate from yourself, thereby extending the life of your business past your own lifetime. Although corporations are often perceived as protection against business liability and a way to protect personal assets from business debt, as an officer of the corporation you are still responsible for its acts; and most banks will require your personal guarantee on a loan to the corporation.

Once upon a time there were tax benefits to being incorporated, but the Tax Reform Act of 1986 eliminated most of those. In some cases, corporate tax rates are higher than individual tax rates. Essentially, your business earnings will be doubly taxed. You will be paid a salary by the corporation on which you will pay personal income taxes. The corporation must pay taxes as well.

Incorporating is a wise move when the business must raise large amounts of capital on a regular basis. Real estate and construction companies are good examples of businesses that need to be incorporated. There are filing fees to be paid and articles of incorporation to be drawn.

A Subchapter S corporation is a hybrid of regular corporations and sole proprietorships. "S corporations," as they are known, pay no corporate income taxes. Earnings are passed on to shareholders in proportion to their ownership, which can be an advantage in states where the individual tax rate is lower than the corporate tax rate. A similar, newer noncorporate form of organization is called a "limited-liability company" (LLC). As with an S corporation, an LLC allows the company income to flow through to its members. To use an LLC, your state must have passed legislation authorizing this form of business organization.

The benefits of corporate status versus sole proprietorship

should be discussed in detail with your legal adviser. Here are some thoughts on the topic from Paul and Sarah Edwards, authors of *Working from Home*.

> A reason for incorporating that can overshadow all other considerations is to preserve your self-employment status for tax purposes. If your work is such that you work for a few clients during a year or are in an industry being targeted by the IRS for making employees out of independent contractors, a newer and better reason to incorporate yourself is to preserve your self-employment status and avoid being classified as a common-law employee by the Internal Revenue Service or a state revenue agency. Further, if you work for companies who fear working with you as an independent contractor might make them vulnerable to costly penalties and back taxes if you are reclassified as a common-law employee, your ability to market yourself may depend on being incorporated. . . .
>
> Being employed by your corporation may enable you to obtain workers' compensation for yourself as a form of disability insurance. A corporation may have advantages for you for sheltering retirement benefits if your net income is high enough. It also offers better opportunities for raising capital if you choose to expand your business. . . . One reason that prompts some to incorporate is that appearing to be employed, even though the employer is your own corporation, may make it easier to obtain credit or buy a home or a car.
>
> On the other side of the ledger, corporations are much more expensive to start. They involve extensive paperwork and record keeping, are closely regulated, and may be subject to double taxation because some states do not recognize S corporations. This means you may be paying state corporate taxes as well as state and federal individual income taxes.

According to the Edwardses, of the 428,000 attorneys listed in the yellow pages in the United States, 256,000 filed sole proprietorship tax returns and 126,000 were covered by partnership returns in 1991. Only about 10 percent of the nation's attorneys—the very people whose advice you would seek on incorporation—have incorporated their own businesses.

Since I've already broached the taxing subject of taxation, let's investigate what your tax reporting and paying responsibilities will be as a business owner.

# Federal and State Income Taxes

For the most part, companies that pay you for your services will request your social security number and report what they have paid you to the IRS on Form 1099. They are obliged to file these by January 31 of the year following each year in which they paid at least $600, and to send you a copy of the form by that date.

Similarly, any subcontractors you pay—writers, editors, artists, illustrators, graphic designers, photographers, and the like—will need a completed Form 1099 from you by January 31 of the year following each year in which they were paid at least $600 by you.

You are also required to make quarterly estimated payments of your taxes on April 15, July 15, October 15, and January 15 with IRS Form 1040-ES. States that collect income tax have similar forms and also require quarterly estimated payments of state income taxes. If you (and if you are married, your spouse) do not make timely payments totaling at least 110 percent of your previous year's tax liability into the federal and state treasury before April 15, and you owe money, you will be assessed stiff penalties for underpayment of taxes. If your spouse works and is not self-employed, you may opt to have additional money withheld from his or her paycheck to cover your combined tax liability.

You must keep accurate and complete records of your revenue and expenses. You can be penalized for overreporting income as well as underreporting income. If you fail to take all the deductions to which you are entitled, then you will pay more self-employment tax than you should, which will result in higher social security (FICA) payments to you someday. The Treasury Department doesn't like that.

Your tax liability could be greater now that you're working for yourself. The net income of your business will be taxed as your personal income by both state and federal governments. Plus, you will pay self-employment tax of 15.3 percent on your business bottom line. This is in lieu of the 7.65 percent FICA payments that were withheld—and matched—by your employer. That is one good reason to take all the deductions to which you are entitled. For every dollar on your bottom line, 15.3 cents will be subtracted for self-employment tax. (One-half of your self-employment liability is then subtracted from your income on the front page of your Form 1040, resulting in a lower adjusted gross income figure.)

If you have a working spouse, your income will be subject to the "marriage penalty." My part-time business profit is added to my spouse's full-time salary and taxed at the top rate. When I factor state and self-employment income taxes into the picture, I pay nearly 50 percent of my profit in taxes.

That is why I take every deduction to which I am entitled. I deduct space for an office in my home, because I have an office which was built exclusively for use by my business.

## The Home Office Deduction

Your home office does not have to be a separate room. It could be an alcove, a portion of a spare bedroom, or other space, but in order to be deductible as a home office it must be used *regularly and exclusively* for business and must be *the the place where the most important work of the business is done.* In a recent Supreme Court decision, an anesthesiologist was denied the home office deduction even though he had no other office because the Court said his most important work was done in the operating room. Although he did all his business record keeping and billing in his home office, it was not considered his principal place of work. This ruling affects home-based business people, such as consultants, who do their "most important" work outside their office. This ruling should not have an effect on the typical communications company's eligibility for the home office deduction.

Many accountants are conservative by nature. One of my accountants in the early years of my business advised me not to take a home office deduction because it increased my chances of being audited. I listened to him, and I was audited anyway. The fact is, home businesses are targeted for audit by the IRS. (When all was said and done, they owed me money.) Then I met a more assertive tax adviser and she recommended I file amended returns for all the years in which I did not claim a home office deduction. (You may not file amended returns for more than three years prior.) It was a tedious task, but it resulted in a tidy little refund check just when a new baby was arriving and the funds were much needed.

But wait, there's more. By claiming a home office deduction, when you sell your house, you cannot "roll over" the portion of the sale that is attributable to your home office space. You must pay capital gains taxes on it.

For example, say you purchased your home for $50,000 and made $20,000 in qualifying improvements, for a "basis" of $70,000, and that you regularly claim a 10 percent home office deduction. If you sell your house for $100,000 and buy a more expensive one, there ordinarily would be no capital gains tax due. But in this case 10 percent of your $30,000 gain, or $3,000, is subject to capital gains tax as the portion of your home used for business.

There is one way around this capital gains tax, and that is if you were not entitled to claim the home office deduction for the year in which you sell your home. You would have to move your office out and rent space elsewhere to fit through this loophole. Before you go to such trouble, have your tax adviser crunch some numbers to see just how much capital gains tax you'll owe. It may be more costly to avoid the capital gains tax than to pay it.

For most people, the tax benefit received from the home office deduction is greater than the capital gains tax due on sale. Use the information provided here to discuss with your tax adviser your eligibility for the home office deduction and what you must do to meet the test of regular and exclusive use.

## Automobile Expenses

Another good reason to take the home office deduction is to be able to deduct the use of your automobile from the time you leave home on work-related travel. If you do not take the deduction, then your business mileage begins only after you reach your principal place of work.

The business use of an auto must be more than 50 percent of its total use for it to qualify for depreciation and expense deductions. If you use an automobile 50 percent or less, you can still deduct your mileage at 29 cents per mile (as of 1994). In either case, you must keep meticulous records, in a separate log, of your business mileage and the business purpose of each trip.

If you do qualify to deduct the actual expenses rather than just mileage, here are the expenses that qualify.

- Depreciation (Over five years, you can deduct the percentage of the purchase price that applies to business use. This is a significant figure if you buy a new car.)
- Insurance
- Registration and license plates
- Personal property tax, if any
- Repairs and maintenance, including car washes
- Parking fees and tolls
- Auto club membership

Remember, you must keep all your receipts, deduct only that portion of the expense that applies to business use of your car, and keep an accurate log of your business travel.

## Automobile Leasing

If you lease an automobile, then you can deduct the lease payment to the extent the automobile is used in business. Example: Your lease payment is $400 per month; 75 percent of your automobile use is attributable to business. You can deduct $300 per month, or $3,600 per year, plus 75 percent of all related automobile expenses (insurance, maintenance, repair, and so on).

In some cases, leasing an automobile can offer greater tax benefits than purchasing. To know which is better for you, you'll need to project how much driving you'll actually be doing and what your deductions will be either way.

## Start-up Expenses

The IRS considers any money you spend before you're actually operating your business to be a capital expense not deductible in the current tax year. Some start-up expenses can be deducted over sixty months as long as you file an election to amortize them on Form 4562. If you do not file a Form 4562, you cannot recover these expenses until you sell or close the business.

Such start-up expenses might include

- Attending seminars and workshops on starting a business
- The cost of research publications, such as this book
- Legal and other professional fees for forming a corporation, writing a business plan, conducting market research, and so on
- Fees for business licenses and registering a trade name
- Travel for securing customers and contracts

## Office Equipment

Under Section 179 of the U.S. Tax Code, you can deduct up to $17,500 per year for furnishings and equipment purchased to use in your business. Equipment purchases by the typical home-based business will usually fall below that limit. If the furnishings and equipment have a useful life of at least three years, then you can elect to depreciate them rather than deduct the full amount in the year purchased. (Ask your accountant about IRS guidelines for the amount of time over which particular kinds of equipment can be deducted.)

Whether to "expense" or depreciate equipment is a strategic decision. If you're just starting up and your income is low, you may want to depreciate over a period of years to have more deductions in the future when you'll have more income. Section 179 expense deductions cannot be used to create a business loss that reduces other tax liability. When a business loss would occur, depreciation is the wisest course to take.

For most start-up businesses, the depreciation deduction amounts to a substantial reduction in profit and, hence, tax liability. You may also depreciate or deduct furnishings and equipment that you take from personal use and put into business use. You must, of course, place a fair value on them for tax purposes. Original receipts for the purchase of such equipment will help you to do that.

As with an automobile, if a piece of equipment, such as a computer, is not used solely for business, then you must keep detailed records of business usage to substantiate your deduction. In the case of a computer, you should keep both business and personal time logs.

Also, as with an automobile, an equipment lease may be preferable to buying equipment. This is especially so if you are going to upgrade equipment every year or two and you don't want to be stuck trying to sell used equipment. A lease may also be more attractive if you do not want to lay out the money for equipment up front and the monthly lease payments are lower than the loan payments would be on a financed purchase.

In *Working from Home,* Paul and Sarah Edwards say to read any lease or rental contract thoroughly and realize that everything in the contract is negotiable. Most people make the mistake of believing a big company's contract is a fixed, immovable thing. But, say the Edwardses, everything is negotiable, from the price of the equipment to the interest rate charged and the number of payments. If you're dealing with a store, a salesperson, or a division trying to meet a sales quota, everything could be up for grabs. Learn to be a shrewd negotiator.

## Other Deductions

You may deduct 100 percent of the business costs listed below.

- Bank charges on a business checking account

- Annual fees for credit cards used exclusively for business
- Interest on business debt
- Membership dues for nonprofit professional and business organizations
- Attorneys' and accountants' fees for advice and services related to your business
- Line charges and user fees for on-line research
- Books, journals, magazines, and newspapers that help you manage your business or advance your knowledge of your clients' operations. (I subscribe to newspapers or magazines in every area in which I have active clients to keep apprised of the issues they face.)
- A business telephone line and business use of your personal phone
- The cost of cleaning your office
- Furnishings and decor for your home office (but not wall-to-wall carpeting, light fixtures, or anything else "attached" that will stay with the home)
- Office supplies
- Supplies for refreshments served to clients
- Travel to meet with clients, solicit prospective clients, or participate in seminars or meetings related to your business
- Seminar fees and other educational expenses related to maintaining and improving your professional skills
- Advertising and marketing expenses
- Postage and shipping
- "Casual" labor: Someone you hire from time to time to enter names in your computer database or to help with your filing. You must file a Form 1099 for each person at the end of the year (see page 75).
- The cost of a briefcase and a portfolio
- Bad debts (uncollectable invoices) and casualty losses (to the extent not reimbursed by insurance). *[Note:* These are deductible only if you use the *accrual* method of accounting, not the cash method.]
- Business insurance premiums and the portion of your homeowner's premium allocated to your home office
- Business license fees and taxes

- Costs of securing copyrights, patents, and registered trademarks
- Client gifts, up to $25 per client per gift

You may deduct 50 percent of these business expenses:

- Business meals (document the business purpose of the meal)
- Client entertainment (document the clients in attendance and the business nature of discussion)
- Self-employment taxes (under "adjustments to income" on Form 1040)

As of April 1995, self-employed people may deduct 25 percent of their paid health insurance premiums. This is a deduction from gross income, not a business expense.

You may not deduct:

- Child-care expenses (use regular child-care credits available to all workers)
- Clothing you wear for business
- Landscaping or yard maintenance expenses for your home

Finally, remember, the tax laws are constantly changing. Your best investment is a good tax adviser and a subscription to publications such as *Home Office Computing* that regularly address the changes in tax laws.

## Collecting Taxes

Here's a twist on the tax laws for businesses. You're not just responsible for paying taxes but, in some cases, for collecting them. Check into your state sales tax laws to learn if you will be required to apply for and receive a tax number and charge sales and use tax on your services.

In Michigan, where Wordwerks operates, there is no tax on services that do not result in a finished, tangible product delivered to the client. (So writing, designing, and consulting are not taxable.) But if a communications business arranges for printing and delivers a finished, printed product to a customer in the state of Michigan, it must charge and collect 6 percent sales tax on the entire invoice. Every quarter a sales tax return is due to the state treasury along with a check for the sales tax collected. If a finished product that was produced in Michigan is shipped out of state, no sales taxes are charged.

Some states charge service and use taxes even on writing and consulting services. Contact your state treasury or sales tax bureau to investigate your state's sales tax laws. And if you live in a large city that levies its own sales tax, check into your city-sales-tax-collecting responsibilities as well.

# Your Pension Fund

It is difficult in the early phase of a new business even to think about such things as saving for the future, when every dollar that isn't necessary to live on is rolled back into the business to keep it going. But a simplified employee pension, known as a SEP-IRA, is a tax-sheltered investment in your own peace of mind. On those occasions when I'm biting my nails over a past-due payment from a client, I take comfort in knowing I have my little—but growing—cushion set aside.

You can start a SEP-IRA by filling out a Form 5305-SEP. Any bank or mutual fund company with whom you are establishing an account will help you with the paperwork. You may make a tax-deferred contribution to a SEP-IRA, by April 15, equal to 13.04 percent of your net self-employment earnings from the previous year. Your net earnings are the amount of earnings on which you pay self-employment tax, less the self-employment tax. The IRS limits your SEP contribution to the lesser of $30,000 or 13.04 percent of your net self employment earnings. Once you set up a SEP-IRA, you are not required to put the maximum in it each year. In fact, you can skip a payment altogether.

Another form of pension available to the home-based businessperson is a Keogh retirement plan. It allows you to set aside up to 20 percent of net self-employment earnings, up to $30,000 a year. Keogh paperwork is more complicated than SEP-IRA paperwork and most people need professional help in setting up this type of pension plan.

# Laws, Licensing, and Regulation

In many communities you can take out a business license at town or city hall, or the county courthouse, simply by filling out a form and paying a small fee. In some locales, this will protect your business name from being used by another, but that's not a guarantee everywhere. If the locale where you operate levies taxes on business property, this will put you on the tax rolls for that purpose. It is difficult to discuss business licensing in a general-use book, because the regulations and practices vary from state to state, even from town to town.

Call your town clerk, city hall, and, if applicable, county clerk to learn what is required of businesses in your area. If you have a difficult time getting information, check with your local chamber of commerce, your state or U.S. representative's office, and a regional Small Business Administration office for help tracking down what is required of you. You won't want to invest significantly in a business and then find out you cannot operate it as you intended because you didn't organize it according to local rules and regulations.

## Zoning Laws

One of the most common mistakes home-based business owners make is not checking out their local zoning laws to see if they can operate a home business legally in their area. Nine out of ten communities restrict home-based businesses in some way.

In some areas, you must apply for and receive a zoning variance before you can even plug in a computer. Most communities with zoning ordinances regulate or prohibit exterior signs and look askance at home businesses that "change the character of the neighborhood" by increasing traffic and parking congestion. Visit the zoning official in your community and request a copy of the zoning ordinances for your neighborhood. Read them carefully to determine if you are prohibited from:

- Erecting a sign
- Allowing clients to park on the street
- Hiring workers who come to your home to perform their duties

## Copyrights and Registered Trademarks

One way to build value in a service business is to create a product from your services that has a shelf life and an intrinsic value. For example, if you develop a certain type of survey for one client that could be generic to many clients, you can copyright that survey and sell it as a "product" to other clients. If you develop a computerized survey program, you can copyright that. (Make sure your client understands that you own the survey you are being paid to conduct and that the client owns only the results.)

To obtain copyright information, write the United States Copyright Office, Library of Congress, Washington, DC 20559, or call (202) 707-3000 and ask for information packet number 118.

If you develop a specific product or service and give it a name, or if you want to protect the name of your business, you can claim it as your own unique property by referring to it in printed materials with a superscript TM (for products) or SM (for services). This does not give you the complete legal protection you would get from a registered trademark or service mark. To register your trademark or service mark, write the U.S. Patent and Trademark Office, Washington, DC 20231, or call (703) 308–HELP for the appropriate forms and instructions.

# Business Insurance

In general, you should attempt to minimize the risk to the business resources and activities that keep you in business and whose loss—even temporarily—would keep you from conducting normal business and earning a living. One way to do this is to prevent loss by staying healthy, avoiding high-risk behavior, and keeping your auto and business equipment in good repair. Another way is to purchase insurance protection. Policies and riders that protect your assets and your earning ability include

- Auto insurance, specifically personal liability and property damage protection
- Health insurance
- Disability and loss-of-income insurance on you
- Theft and casualty insurance for your business property
- Business interruption insurance
- Liability insurance for the actions of your business
- Insurance covering data stored in your computer

Many home-based-business owners mistakenly believe that their existing home and auto policies will sufficiently protect their business as well. In fact, most policies exclude business use of your home. Consult with your insurance agent to make sure you are covered if

- Your business computers and other equipment are stolen or damaged by fire or water
- Your business operations—and your earning ability—are interrupted due to fire or weather damage to your home (and if you live in an earthquake or flood zone, those risks as well).
- Your hard drive crashes and erases important data
- A client, supplier, or courier gets hurt when visiting your property
- An illness or injury prevents you from working and earning money

Business insurance can be costly. In the start-up phase of your business, try to strike a balance between what you need and what you can afford. Additional riders on your homeowner's and auto policies may be sufficient to minimize your risks.

## Health Insurance

If you have no health insurance, the National Association for the Self-Employed (NASE) offers reasonably priced health coverage for its members. To inquire about membership benefits, write NASE Information Services, P.O. Box 869023, Plano, TX 75086–9899.

If you are leaving the employ of a company that paid your health insurance, you have a statutory right to continue the same coverage for a nominal fee for up to eighteen months. Check with the benefits administrator at your current or former employer for details.

## Disability Insurance

According to the insurance industry, about half of all workers become disabled—meaning unable to work—either permanently or temporarily during their work lives. If the income you earn from your home-based profession is essential to your survival, and if your absence from the office owing to illness or injury would reduce or eliminate that income, then you probably need to purchase some amount of disability insurance.

Premiums vary depending on the amount of monthly income you are insuring, the percentage of that income you would be paid in the event of a disability, the length of time after the onset of the disability before benefits begin, and the duration of payments.

Here's an example of a "no frills" minimal coverage policy that might be a good choice for someone just starting out in business. For about $200 per year, the policy will pay about $1,000 per month for one year, beginning sixty days after the onset of disability. This is minimal protection, but it's also at a minimum cost. As your business and income grow, you can choose to purchase more coverage as you can afford it.

## Business Property and Income Insurance

There is a wide variety of home business coverages available, at costs ranging from a few hundred to several thousand dollars a year. Prices also vary depending on where your home is located and what risk factors exist.

In my area, basic risk protection is available for a reasonable price. For about only $150 per year, a policy provides

- $10,300 of theft and fire coverage for business computers and furnishings
- $300,000 per incident of liability coverage (up to $600,000 per year)
- $5,000 in medical payments per person for accidents and injuries sustained on your premises
- Payments to replace lost revenue resulting from normal business operations being interrupted by a fire, theft, or other covered casualty loss.

In addition, policies are available to cover the cost of re-creating data and restoring system use when you experience a hard-drive crash, virus, or other computer system failure. According to my insurance agent, the cost for such a policy in my area through State Farm is $1.50 per year for each $100 of coverage. So for $150 a year, you can purchase $10,000 in coverage to protect your communications company's lifeblood: computers and information.

For any insurance purchase, shop around for the best price and investigate the company before buying. Ask for references from other business owners and review published ratings of the companies you are considering. A good rule of thumb is, if you cannot afford to lose it, insure it. Just don't cripple your business with huge premium payments you don't need right now.

# Record Keeping

Most start-up businesses have minimal bookeeping demands at first, which is why most home-based business people wait to install record-keeping software on their computers. That's unfortunate because, according to the magazine *Home Office Computing*, 40 percent of small businesses never make the switch. As their businesses grow, they devote more and more management time to keeping track of numbers and developing reports that could be done effortlessly—and far more effectively—by the right accounting or bookkeeping program. For a fraction of the cost of a bookkeeping service, such programs can provide sophisticated financial-management assistance. The time to install one, however, is at the beginning, before the press of business prevents you from devoting the time.

According to *Home Office Computing* ("Making Sense of Your Dollars," November 1993), here's what your accounting system should offer you.

*A Profit and Loss Statement:* The program will add up all of your income, subtract all of your expenses, and then tell you what's left.

*A Balance Sheet:* This tells you what your business owns and owes. For a one-person service business, expect both parts to be small. But if you find yourself with a negative balance sheet, look carefully to make sure you aren't overextending yourself on debt that your business can't pay for.

*A Cash Budget:* How much money came in and went out this month? What do you expect next month? Will you make enough in sales this year to pay for a new copier and part-time assistant? You can be profitable but lack cash flow, and that can be deadly for a fledgling business.

*A Tax Report:* Buy a program (or set one up yourself) that tracks your expenses by tax category. So at year's end, you know how much you spent on deductible advertising, supplies, and the like.

*The Divisional Data That Drives Decisions:* If you provide more than one kind of good or service or service more than one kind of customer, try to find a system that lets you code them. Then you can massage the numbers when you make your long-range plans and focus on those parts of your business that earn the most. You may be spinning wheels for clients who aren't paying you enough to cover axle grease while your more profitable clients are being overlooked.

*A Regular Reality Check:* Maybe you're spending $60 for every $75 you bring in—or even more. If you're running your business in such a direction, that is a big mistake. The numbers won't lie. On the other hand, maybe you're feeling unnecessarily gloomy. An accounting system should be able to reassure you that, "Yes, October was a bad month last year, too" or "Look at how much money you've made this year."

*A Comfortable Feeling:* Find a program that fits your computing and accounting style. If you are comfortable with debits and credits within the traditional accounting environment, find a program that looks and acts like a ledger. If all of the above makes you nervous, find a program that masks the jargon. Pick a system that requires the kind of commitment you're willing to make in terms of time, training, and effort.

*Depending on the nature of your business, you'll want programs that can handle the following as well.*

*Accounts Receivable:* If you invoice for your services, you'll want a program that does it for you. It should print invoices, track what's owed you, and age the invoices (automatically note second notices and tell you how long you're owed some money). If you work hourly, consider the programs that will keep your hours and automatically bill them.

*Inventory:* A good program will tell you what you have left, when do you need to order more, and print out the purchase order with the appropriate supplier's name.

*Payroll:* This is a headache unto itself of withholding percentages and legal requirements. A good payroll program (some are stand-alone and operate independently of your main bookkeeping and accounting program) will come with state tax tables and alleviate the headaches.

(Reprinted by permission from *Home Office Computing* magazine © 1993. For subscription information, call 800-288-7812.)

Some businesses are simple enough that a personal finance, or checkbook, program such as Quicken can suffice. While these keep track of money in and money out, and print your checks, they typically don't allow you to generate invoices automatically or keep track of inventory.

The next step up is small-business bookkeeping software, such as QuickBooks or BestBooks. These fulfill the accounting needs of small businesses, including sales analysis and project management, without requiring a CPA license to understand them. They don't include payroll, however, and inventory control tools are often lacking. If you plan to grow beyond a business of one, you might look into small-business accounting programs such as M.Y.O.B. or Peachtree Accounting for Windows. These allow inventory management, provide aged receivable reports, and will basically give you a report and a bottom-line amount for just about anything. This type of program will require more setup time and has a longer learning curve. Familiarity with accounting jargon, if not methods, is helpful.

## What's in a Name?

Now, there's one more thing to consider before putting the finishing touches on your start-up business plan—and that's your name. In my case, the easiest decision I had was what to name my business. I am first and foremost a writer, so words are my stock in trade. That in combination with my unique surname led me easily to Wordwerks, which has always worked well for me. In the early days I was "Wordwerks Publications Services," but as I expanded my writing and production management services to include marketing and communications consulting, "Wordwerks Communications" was a better fit.

You may have already named your business. If not, make sure the name you choose reflects, briefly and straightforwardly, what you want potential clients to know about you. Your business name is an important marketing tool. It should be easy to spell, pronounce, and remember.

Many people use their last names, as in "Saunders Communications." That works especially well if the owner's past experience gives him or her instant name recognition with potential clients. If not, it's a pretty broad umbrella of a title.

If you've selected a specialty as recommended in chapter 2, perhaps your business name can reflect it. Will you specialize in marketing research using focus groups and surveys? Then perhaps a name such as "Customer Connections" with a subhead "Customized Research That Gets Results" on your marketing materials will work.

Here are some strong words to use in communications company titles.

| | |
|---|---|
| Solutions | Quality |
| Resources | Creative |
| Support | Unique |
| Ideas | Target |
| Intelligence | Realistic |
| Advantage | Effective |
| Image | |

# Assembling the Business Plan

Now it's time to assemble your start-up business plan. Here again is the outline (from chapter 3, pages 63–65). Begin each section on a new page.

## 1. Executive Summary

Write a paragraph that summarizes the business plan. Include name of business, business address, form of organization, target market, and main business activities. Be as specific and concrete as you can. Here's an example.

Health-Link Communications, a sole proprietorship operating at [business address], specializes in effective customer communications for health-care providers and the businesses that serve them. Owner and director [name of owner] is a successful writer, editor, and health-care marketing professional who combines her extensive knowledge of written communications with unique survey tools to create and produce newsletters, brochures, direct-mail programs, and other print communications that improve relationships with customer groups and enhance the bottom line.

Health-Link is a full-service company, offering clients the convenience of start-to-finish production management. Low overhead combined with excellent long-term relationships with carefully screened vendors allow Health-Link to deliver top-quality print products to its clients at a fraction of the fees charged by large advertising and communications agencies.

## 2. Resumés of Owners

In one page if possible, two at the most, include a polished, professional resumé that lists in inverse chronological order (most to least recent) the positions you've held. For each position, describe briefly the accomplishments and results that will be useful in the business specialty you've chosen. If the business is a partnership or corporation, include resumés for all partners or officers and directors. If you have examples of work you've done that are similar to work you'll be doing for clients, you can include these in a special appendix.

## 3. Business Structure/Form of Organization

If you will operate as a sole proprietorship, the following statement will suffice:

"XYZ Communications" is a sole proprietorship owned and operated by [name of owner] at [business address] and complying with all laws, regulations, and restrictions that govern home-based occupations in [name of city], [name of county], [name of state].

If your business is a partnership, in addition to the business name and address, name all partners, gives their titles, describe their respective roles in the management of the business, and list each party's partnership interest (what percentage of the business each partner owns).

If you are a corporation:

"Communique, Incorporated," is a corporation organized under the laws of the state of [name of state] on [date] and having its principal place of business at [business address].

List names and titles of officers and directors of the corporation and show each person's ownership interest. Include a copy of the "Articles of Incorporation and Bylaws" as a separate appendix. Refer to it in this section.

For all types of business organization, include in this section a page titled "Professional Advisers." On this page list the names and addresses of legal advisors, accounting firms, consultants, and others whose professional services you've used to help you develop your business. This will show your banker you mean business.

## 4. Financial Statements

Construct your financial statements using the data you assembled and entered on worksheets in chapter 3. You may want to have your accountant prepare these under the accounting firm's letterhead, just to add credibility. Even if you don't, it is wise to have your accountant review your financial statements.

*Personal Financial Statement:* Construct your own personal financial statement from the worksheet in chapter 3, pages 66–67.

*Personal Income Statement:* This outlines the owner's personal living expenses less other sources of income. Rename the "Personal Budget Worksheet" from pages 40–41 in chapter 3 and include it here.

*Business Start-up Expenses:* The "Start-up Equipment and

Supplies Costs" Worksheet (page 54) and the "Start-up Marketing and Promotion Costs Worksheet" (page 55) can be combined to produce this document.

*Business Cash Flow Projections:* While the "Business Cash Flow Projections Worksheet" (page 57) will work here, a six-month or one-year spreadsheet, showing income figures increasing each month, would be preferable.

*Total Start-up Capital Being Sought:* Rename and plug in your completed "Recap Worksheet" from chapter 3, page 58, here.

### Start-up Capital Needs

| | |
|---|---|
| Monthly personal expenses times six months | $ _____ |
| Start-up costs: equipment and supplies | $ _____ |
| Start-up costs: marketing and promotion | $ _____ |
| Projected monthly business overhead expense times six months: | $ _____ |
| Total needed | $ _____ |

## 5. Marketing Plan

From chapter 2 (page 36), plug in your marketing plan. You can flesh out this basic plan with specific promotions, schedules, and costs. You may wish to wait to complete this section of your plan until after you've read chapter 6, which focuses on marketing and promotion.

## Let's Get Going!

If you're a typical entrepreneur with a creative bent (and if you're not, why have you read this far?), you're probably chomping at the bit to get going. And that's just what you're going to do, starting with chapter 5. Planning and organization are vital to your eventual success, but now it's time to move on to the details of running your new business. It's time, in other words, to hit the road. We have places to go and people to see. Fasten your seat belt.

## Marketing Plan: Revised Version

Name of business:

Name of owner:

Owner's background, experience, and accomplishments:

Description of services and products:

Target clients and industries:

Differential advantage (how I will add value to my customers' organizations):

Marketing and promotion plans:

# 5

# Getting Out and Doing It

## Simple Systems for Success

In the introduction to this book I wrote that the first reaction I usually get when I tell people I operate a home-based business is, "How lucky you are to work at home!" The second thing they usually say is, "I don't know where you get the discipline to work when you're all by yourself."

I don't know a single successful home-based businessperson who has difficulty mustering the motivation to work. Most of the people I know have more work than they can possibly handle in the hours they have allotted to work. We all end up spending more time than we said we would at the office. So systems for getting work in and getting work out, for making sure that you and your clients are on the same wavelength about project objectives and scope, and for handling essential record keeping and administrative tasks are essential.

The response I'd like to give, but never have, to the person who wonders how I get motivated to work is, "Then I don't recommend you ever start your own business." For the rest of you, who will have more work than you have hours to accomplish it all, this chapter contains some simple, successful systems to help you wear all the hats you must wear in a given day.

# Build, Don't Burn, Bridges

One of the first and most important tasks of a new entrepreneur is to get the word out about the new business. Your current professional contacts are likely to be a significant source of clients and client referrals. If you're still working for someone else, however, you may face a delicate balancing act. You may not want your current employer to discover your self-employment plans out of concern that you'll be asked to leave before you're ready. It's certainly not an unfounded fear.

Many home-based business owners moonlight part time until they feel comfortable letting go of that regular paycheck. Some do it openly, others secretly. Here's one (failed) business owner's advice about keeping your business plans a secret (it's from "Autopsy of a Business" by Judith Gross, *Home Office Computing,* October 1993).

> The concept I had with my friend (whom I'll call Jeff) was to publish a twice-monthly newsletter on a new digital technology being proposed for the nation's 12,000-odd radio stations and sell subscriptions to radio station managers, researchers promoting the new technology, lobbyists, lawyers, and government organizations.
>
> It seemed to me that the topic for our publishing venture was hot and that sooner or later someone else would have the same idea. Jeff, who was in a related business, said that secrecy should be our code until we launched.
>
> I see now that our enjoyment of our little secret somehow carried us away from the sobering tasks of launching a new business. For one thing, it isolated me from others who had started similar businesses who might have given me different advice. But ultimately, the consequences proved much more severe to my own career.
>
> I worked for a successful publisher and businessman who respected my talents, trusted me, and had promoted me to a management position. The smart thing would have been to get his advice and learn from his 15 years of expertise.
>
> I also could have taken the opportunity to feel him out on how becoming publisher of my own newsletter (which was

not in conflict with his publications, although it was in a related industry) would affect my five-year relationship with his company.

When we finally revealed the launch of the newsletter—the day the first issue mailed—my employer felt betrayed and all but fired me. In the end, I negotiated an out-basis consultancy, which paid me far less than I could afford to live on. By default, I became a salaried employee of my newly formed corporation.

(Used with permission of the author.)

This rueful would-be business owner learned the hard way that secrecy can exact too high a price. Rather than burning her bridges, she should have used the goodwill of her long-term relationship with her current employer to build a bridge to self-employment success.

Now, I know from personal experience that some employers simply don't operate by reason. The minute they hear of any employee making other career plans, they treat it as treason. In a business such as communications and marketing, such fears may be grounded in the fact that employees often do leave and take clients with them.

I would never recommend starting a business based on wooing away your employer's clients. That's another one of those business beasts that comes back to bite you in the behind someday. If you suspect that your business plans will get out, or if you would like the goodwill and support of your colleagues in your new venture, then share your plans and your timetable with your employer. Let your current colleagues know that you're not interested in the firm's clients, but that you hope they will refer business to you if they can. You may work out a suitable arrangement for handling your company's overflow. They may even have a client or two they'd rather send your way. You could embark on your business venture with a built-in client base and a positive cash flow.

I have seen home-based businesses get under way with work from clients of their former employers, and in every such situation the former employer was a business that was on its way out

of business owing to mismanagement. These were all cases of as-
tute employees reading the handwriting on the wall and making
plans accordingly.

Whatever decisions you make, strive to keep contacts in-
tact—and on your side. Success in the marketing and communications business is based on who you know and what they think
of you as much as it is based on what you know and how well
you deliver services.

# Your Start-up Marketing Kit

Now that you know your business name, specialty, and target
market, it's time to let prospective clients know. In order to do
that you need a few basic tools:

- a telephone
- business cards
- letterhead, envelopes, and labels
- a capabilities brochure
- a list of prospective clients

## Phone and Mail

Now get out there and communicate. Begin by making a list of
everyone you already know who could be a client or might refer
you to a client. Mail each a brochure with a cover letter and business card. Follow each letter up with a personal telephone call.

## Business and Professional Groups

Make another list of every other prospective client or source of
client referrals. Follow the same mail/phone procedure. If you're
targeting local businesses, join your local chamber of commerce
and other business organizations in your area. Just don't spend
all your time going to breakfast and lunch meetings. Target your
market and focus your efforts where they will pay off.

# A Newsletter

Publish your own communications newsletter and mail it to your prospect list. This is a clever and relatively inexpensive way to get a sample of your work in front of prospective clients. Make it good! Fill it full of useful information, statistics, and survey results on communications, on your clients' particular industry (if applicable), and on your services, and be sure your telephone number and logo are prominently located on each page. As your business grows, include your own success stories about projects you've undertaken with clients (with their permission, of course). If that won't work, simply include a "new clients this quarter" feature or listing.

## Business Seminars and Expos

Call local business groups and ask if any are planning a "business expo" in the future. Inquire about show dates, format, and cost of booth rental. Instead of going to the expense of renting a booth and creating signs and displays, offer to teach a workshop for no charge. It won't cost you anything beyond the cost of materials you hand out, and it will give you a captive audience of potential customers and customer referrals.

## Free Publicity

Send press releases about your business, and black-and-white copies of your professional portrait, to the business editors of local and metropolitan newspapers, magazines, and business journals. Follow up with calls to editors offering your expertise whenever they are working on stories in your field—in exchange for recognition of your business in the article.

## Barter

Exchange your services for the services of others. If you need shelves built, find a carpenter who will do the work in exchange for a brochure or flyer. While this shouldn't be the only work you do, if you set aside one day a week during your start-up period for working on barter arrangements, eventually you'll have a portfolio of finished products to show potential clients, and perhaps some more referrals.

# Productivity Pointers

And now for the subject of balancing the tasks of getting work in and getting work out. I recommend that you develop a system based on the way you work best. I, for example, know that I can produce more copy faster the longer I work. In other words, if I only work an hour here, an hour there on a long project, I'm not very productive. If I have a long newsletter or manual to write, I set aside one or two days for conducting the necessary interviews and collecting the research, and then I put my answering machine on automatic for a couple days and write straight through. My creative skills seem to be at their height after five hours. I usually completely rewrite what I accomplished in the first few hours.

In order to finish all the work I have to do and still be available for client meetings and calls, I try to make and return phone calls early or late in the day. Similarly, I schedule appointments in or out of the office for early in the morning or in the mid-to-late afternoon. I screen my phone calls when I'm working and only take the most critical calls. On those extrabusy days when the phone just won't leave me alone, I often give up and wait until 5:00 p.m. Then, when the phones are silent, provided there's energy left and the creative juices are flowing, I can do the "real work" of my business.

## Project Management

Some people manage work flow using computer programs set up for that purpose. I'm still using systems I devised twenty years ago in the workplace, but they work for me. Find the system that works best for you. Here's how I do it:

Each client has a paper file folder in my file cabinet, as well as a file folder on my computer. In addition to being in my computer database, their phone numbers, addresses, important contact names, and titles are all printed on labels and affixed to the inside front of the paper folder. When a client calls and I pull that file, everything I need to know is right in front of me.

I keep client files I'm currently working on in a standing file holder on my work table, within reach of both computer and phone. Not until the work is completed and invoiced are they refiled in my file cabinet. For ongoing projects, such as monthly and quarterly newsletters, I note in my calendar when to pull the file again and begin work on the next issue. While computer programs are available to do the same thing, my paper-based tickler system seems to work fine for me.

## Invoicing and Collecting Fees

I learned my billing system from my early years as a legal assistant. I keep a piece of lined paper stapled to the inside back cover of every file, and I record date, work done (including meetings and telephone conferences), and number of hours spent as I do the work. At the end of every month, I check that sheet, total the hours, generate invoices, and make a note in the file of the number of hours invoiced. Then I file a copy of each invoice in my "pending invoices" file.

When I file the current month's invoices, I also check for unpaid invoices from the previous month. If an invoice remains unpaid after thirty days, I call the client's accounting department or send a statement, based on what I've learned is the best way to handle that client's billing. I'm happy to say I almost never have to beg for my fees, or even remind clients that an invoice is over thirty days old.

As mentioned in chapter 4, certain small-business accounting programs will tell you as soon as you open them up what invoices remain unpaid. This helps you keep track of how much you have coming in. I, for one, am never happy when there are no pending invoices, because that means there won't be any checks in the mailbox until I send another invoice.

When an invoice is paid, I enter the amount into the program I use for generating monthly and quarterly statements. Then I keep all copies of paid invoices in a file through the end of the year.

If a project will take longer than a month to complete, I always ask clients if I can bill monthly. Most readily assent. All my suppliers bill me monthly, and it is simpler to keep on top of payables and receivables every thirty days than to let it go for longer periods. My clients usually understand that I am spending money on their behalf and nearly all have been cooperative about billing issues.

Perhaps because one of my first jobs was in a law office handling the firm's commercial-credit-collection files, I am not shy about collecting money. Unfortunately, too many small-business owners are reluctant to pick up the phone and call a client about an overdue invoice. As a result, all too often their businesses fail. Don't build your own business on the backs of your suppliers, and don't allow other businesses to do that to you. If a client pays steadily but slowly, you might learn to live with it. If you're spending more time on collections with a client than you did on the actual work, don't work for that client again. There are plenty of others out there who will appreciate you and pay you for your work on time.

## Retainers and Advanced Billing

One of the best ways to handle the billing of work you do regularly is through the negotiation of a monthly retainer arrangement. This evens out your cash flow as well as the client's. I've found this is easiest to do with clients with whom I have established relationships. Once there exists a history of invoices to show the client, you can say: "I've noticed that my fees for work on this publication average $3,000 a quarter, or $1,000 per month. Can we set up an arrangement for an automatic payment of $1,000 to be sent on the fifteenth of each month? I'll send a statement after each publication detailing services and expenses for that quarter. Any additional amounts due can be paid at that time."

With clients whose accounting methods won't allow retainer arrangements, you may be able to smooth out cash flow by billing them when a project begins, rather than when it ends. I do this for all periodicals I produce. The client's total fee for production is negotiated annually.

As an example, here is a typical production schedule for a monthly, four-page newsletter: Research and writing are accomplished from the first through the tenth of the month. The designer has until the seventeenth to finish design work and deliver a disk to the printer, and the printer has until the twenty-fifth to ship. The newsletter is in the client's hands by the thirtieth at the latest. An invoice was sent on the last day of the preceding month, and it comes up in the client's payable cycle on the thirtieth of the current month. The product has been delivered, and the invoice is paid. The suppliers are all paid within thirty days of delivering the work as well.

### Purchase Orders

Some companies will require that you have a purchase order number before you can invoice a project. This usually involves calling the accounting department, or your contact within the company, and giving the amount of the invoice in advance. Ask new clients before you begin work if that is the case. If it is, and you wait until the work is done, your payment could take longer than you'd like. Arrange to get a purchase order number as soon as possible. Even if a P.O. number isn't required, devise your own invoice-numbering system so that you can keep track of invoices and refer to the number when questioning a client about payment. My invoices look like the one shown in the accompanying box.

# Focusing on the Future

It's very tempting when you have client work to do to ignore management and marketing tasks. But you must always look to

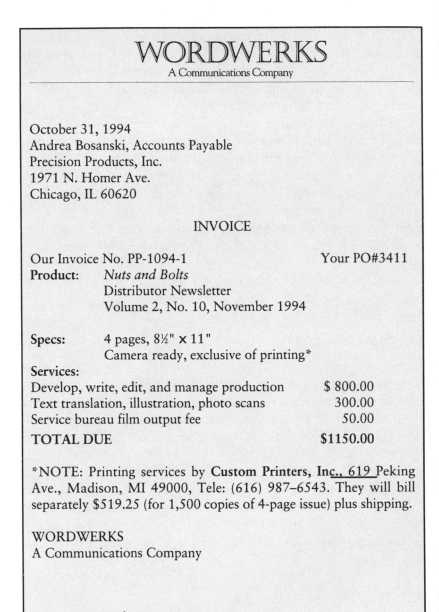

# WORDWERKS
### A Communications Company

October 31, 1994
Andrea Bosanski, Accounts Payable
Precision Products, Inc.
1971 N. Homer Ave.
Chicago, IL 60620

### INVOICE

Our Invoice No. PP-1094-1                    Your PO#3411
**Product:**    *Nuts and Bolts*
                Distributor Newsletter
                Volume 2, No. 10, November 1994

**Specs:**      4 pages, 8½" x 11"
                Camera ready, exclusive of printing*
**Services:**
Develop, write, edit, and manage production      $ 800.00
Text translation, illustration, photo scans       300.00
Service bureau film output fee                     50.00
**TOTAL DUE**                                    **$1150.00**

*NOTE: Printing services by **Custom Printers, Inc., 619** Peking
Ave., Madison, MI 49000, Tele: (616) 987–6543. They will bill
separately $519.25 (for 1,500 copies of 4-page issue) plus shipping.

WORDWERKS
A Communications Company

Louann N. Werksma

**Sample Invoice**

that day when the current projects are done and no new work waits. I recommend scheduling one day a week, be it all day or only a few hours, when you focus on future business.

I keep a file of pending proposals, notes from potential clients who've made inquiries, and businesss cards from people I've met who've expressed an interest in my services. On "marketing day" I make follow-up calls or cold calls and try to set a firm appointment to meet with at least one decision maker to discuss the client's potential communications needs within the next week. Sometimes in those meetings we're able to pinpoint communications solutions the client had not even considered and I walk away with a work order after only one try. Other times it takes months before something comes through. And sometimes it never does. Time spent on clients that never results in billable work is simply a cost of doing business.

## Build a Strong Supplier Network

Another critical management task involves building a network of suppliers who can be there for you when a big project comes in. I usually have a primary graphic designer to whom I funnel the lion's share of my work. But when that designer gets busy, I make sure there are others to call. So I try to make time to meet with graphic designers, writers, illustrators, and photographers, to review their portfolios, discuss the fees they charge, and learn when they are available.

Sometimes these same people refer work to me. On "marketing day," it's good to let your suppliers and colleagues know if you expect some downtime. They may be swamped and need an extra hand.

# The Virtual Agency

Building and maintaining a network of other professionals to back you up can lead to more business and greater profitability. In my case it has allowed me to take on more work than I can actually handle myself in the hours I have available, because there are backup firms to give me a hand. I stay in control of the project, maintain contact with the client, and invoice through my firm, but I share the fees with other firms like mine through an agreement we've already negotiated. Then, when they are busy, they send work my way. It's a whole new twist on competition.

It's been my experience over the past eight years that most people who do what I do aren't competitors. Rather, we're colleagues in a new world of work. Others have coined the term "virtual agency" or "virtual corporation" to refer to people working under separate roofs but with nontraditional employment bonds of their own making. My term for this new system of independent contractors sharing work, contacts, and knowledge is a "co-orporation." We're cooperating for our own success and the good of our client companies. As a result, home-based marketing/communications firms are able to create the same quality product for clients of all sizes, at a much lower price than that charged by large agencies. Madison Avenue has moved to Main Street, and every business in America can now have access to professional marketing and communications expertise at an affordable price.

An article entitled "In Unity There's Profit" by Donna M. Partow in the August 1994 issue of *Home Office Computing* gave home-based businesses important tips on how to accomplish partnering successfully. Here is an excerpt.

> Throughout America, entrepreneurs are creating strategic alliances—a business entity that lies midway between the isolation of sole proprietorship and the potential pitfalls of a standard partnership. Here's how it works: You form a network of associates with complementary talents, knowledge, resources, and skills. You're committed to one another, but you're not legally or financially bound. Together you have the muscle and reach of a larger corporation without overextending yourself with employees, extra paperwork, or overhead.
>
> An increasingly competitive marketplace makes strategic alliances desirable while rapidly advancing technology makes them possible. Meetings are easy with the aid of fax machines, voice mail, cellular phones, pagers, notebook computers, and

modems for data exchange and access to e-mail and online services. *Possible Pitfalls.* The advantages of strategic alliances are readily apparent. You can increase earnings by serving clients landed by alliance members and receive referral fees on business you send their way. And you can accept projects you otherwise would turn down because you lacked the necessary expertise. What's more, you can reduce costs by pooling resources and undertaking joint marketing efforts.

Selecting the wrong alliance member, however, can become a nightmare. Breaking ties will be easier than if you were involved in a full partnership, but your reputation may suffer just as much. You still surrender a certain amount of control: He may drop the ball or fail to perform to your standards. And there's not much you can do—except cut your losses.

Edwin Richard Rigsbee, author of *The Art of Partnering* (Kendall/Hunt), recommends working with a potential member on small projects first. When you're ready to formalize an alliance, spend plenty of time hashing out the terms. "You have to clarify expectations and define your commitment level," notes Rigsbee. "Although I don't recommend a legal contract, it's wise to draft a letter of understanding of a charter. Spell out exactly what each member agrees to do."

(Reprinted by permission from *Home Office Computing* magazine © 1994. For subscription information, call 800-288-7812.)

# On-Line Support

One of the places that co-orporations do their work is in that place known as cyberspace. I mentioned in chapter 3 that your computer modem would be useful for communicating with clients and suppliers and for sending files electronically. But it can also link you to others who can provide services, support, information, and referrals. One on-line service, CompuServe, offers two forums that are helpful resources for the home-based communications business.

## PR and Marketing Forum (PRSIG)

This forum provides a special-interest group for professional communicators in the fields of public relations, marketing, and communications or those holding related jobs in the public and private sector. The data libraries cover a wide variety of topics related to PR, including government, education, public affairs, financial institutions, consumer affairs, computers, high tech, health and social services, and the Public Relations Society of America. The teleconferences enable a member to communicate with recognized communications experts. In addition, the forum may be used to establish meetings by members for specific reasons.

## Working from Home Forum (WORK)

This forum unites those who work from their homes with others who are in similar circumstances. It allows a member to exchange information, make contacts, share resources and solutions to problems, meet other members, and keep up-to-date on the latest home-office management tips, resources, laws, tax benefits, and marketing approaches.

# Agreements and Contracts

In your delight at landing that first big client, don't rush away on the strength of a handshake and start creating. When you first return to your office, take a few minutes to organize your notes and reiterate the terms you discussed in a simple "agreement letter" that you mail to the client with a copy to be signed and returned to you. You will then have a legal contract to enforce if you are not paid; but even more important, a written summary ensures that you and the client have understood each other and have the same expectations about the project at hand.

The accompanying box shows a sample agreement letter.

# WORDWERKS
## A Communications Company

December 10, 1994

Jody B. Saunders
Communications Specialist
Business International Corporation
18000 North Westfield Road
Businessville, OH 40000

Dear Jody:

It was a pleasure meeting with you today and discussing your customer communications program. To confirm the contents of that meeting and the actions we decided upon, I am submitting this "Agreement Letter." Please review it and, if it reflects your understanding of our project plans, kindly sign one copy in the space provided and return it to me in the enclosed, self-addressed envelope.

**Wordwerks Communications of Grand Haven, Michigan,** is engaged to produce for the Business International Corporation a quarterly customer newsletter focusing on client success stories within the client's Midwest region. Entitled *B.I.C. Journal,* it will be published each year in January, April, July, and October.

Format: 4-page 22" x 17", folded to 11" x 17", and folded again to an 8½" x 11" self-mailer, 3 ink colors on glossy stock with original graphics, illustrations and photos.

**Wordwerks will:**

Research and investigate chosen article topics, interview Business International Corporation clients, and write all articles as directed by Jody Saunders and submit article manuscripts for approval as to content.

Design publication logo, department art, and graphics. Visit client locations for photographs as needed. Submit prepress and press proofs for client approval. Ship 1,000 copies of each issue by January 31, April 20, July 15, and October 10, 1995, to Client Mailing Center for mailing.

**Business International Corporation will:**

Provide article list and contact names and telephone numbers by [date]. Create database for mailing.

**Fees**

[Outline fees agreed upon and payment schedule]

### AGREEMENT LETTER

The signatures below indicate our understanding of and agreement to the terms, conditions, fees, and payment schedules as set forth in this letter dated December 10, 1994.

WORDWERKS COMMUNICATIONS

_____

Louann N. Werksma, Director          Date: _____

Business International Corporation

                                     Date: _____
_____
Jody B. Saunders, Communications Specialist
authorized to act on behalf of Business International Corporation

## Sample Agreement Letter

## Subcontractor Agreements

When you subcontract with others whose work will have an effect on your company's image, your client relationships, and your product quality and turnaround time, you should also stipulate all the details of your work arrangement and fees, in writing and in advance. Get references if you can before you begin working with someone else, and try new subcontractors out on small projects first just to see if you like their work style and output before plunging ahead with them.

When I first moved my company from Connecticut to Michigan, I had a difficult time locating new suppliers. I enjoyed comfortable, long-term relationships with my suppliers in Connecticut, and it was simpler and more convenient at first to continue working with them.

My initial attempts to hire local designers and printers were unsuccessful. I stopped in at one printing firm, requested a quote for a publication, and never heard from them. I took a disk to a graphic design firm to translate and design for me, just to see a sample of their work. I never went back. I spent way too much money on telephone, fax, and overnight-courier charges while I continued to hire the services of out-of-state subcontractors.

But eventually I met others and became more connected. An article about my company appeared in a local newspaper, and it mentioned that I was seeking local suppliers. My phone rang off the hook with calls from home-based graphic designers and artists, as well as other writers. I have since "let go" of my former suppliers (reluctantly) and now I happily work with talented, competent people right in my new hometown (or close by).

To develop subcontractors who are there when you need them and who help you look good, make sure you pay them fairly and on time, let them know what to expect and when, don't change the scope of the project without also adjusting their fees accordingly, and try to stay to the schedule (although sometimes that is out of your control) so that when you have a need for last-minute, hurry-up-and-rush work, they will be willing to help you out. And remember them at Christmas and throughout the year with small tokens of gratitude.

# Total Quality Management

Total quality management—now there's a big-business buzz-word, but it's even more important for your small business. You actually have more to lose when a client is not satisfied or a client's project does not go according to plan. Although no one likes to think about problems, they do occur.

When interviewing suppliers, inquire about their policies for making good on errors. I learned this the hard way. My first printer, who was not a good business manager, didn't like to give an inch, even when the mistake occurred on press. After one or two projects came off the press with registration problems or color inconsistencies—and no willingness on the printer's part to make good—I wised up. I found a printing company that rarely made errors but, when they did, made good in a big way. On one occasion, a small photograph on an inside page of a client's newsletter was inadvertently printed upside down. The printer was ready to reprint and reship at its own expense, but the client declined owing to tight mailing schedules. My client wasn't particularly upset, but the printer insisted on printing the entire next issue of the newsletter—1,500 copies—free of charge. The client was delighted and so was I.

The production stage of any communications product, be it print, voice, or video, is critical. Work with people who have integrity, who demonstrate a good business track record, and who are scrupulous about their finished product and willing to stipulate in writing what they will do to correct errors if they occur. By the same token, you should keep a little cushion of cash in your accounts for "make-goods." It could be the difference between keeping a big client and going on—or going under.

# Set Your Priorities

My best advice for the smooth operation of your business is to know your priorities and create a work schedule and simple systems to fulfill them. You don't get paid for having lunch with friends, taking nonbusiness phone calls during work hours, doing housework, running personal errands, or rearranging your desk drawers.

Decide when you will be open for business, let clients know when they can reach you, and learn to screen your calls when you're working on deadline. Be faithful about returning client calls before the end of business on the day they were received if possible, and make sure your friends and family know that you and your office are enshrouded in an invisible cloaking device during work hours. In other words, no unnecessary interruptions. It's not easy, but it is essential to your success.

A smart man I once knew said to me, "The business of business is getting and keeping customers." Coming up in chapter 6 is a collection of time-tested methods for promoting your business, finding clients, and keeping them coming back for more of your unique and effective communications solutions.

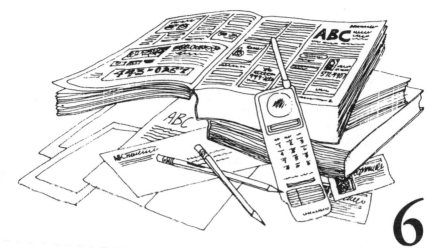

# 6

# Communicator, Communicate Thyself

## Creative, Low-Cost Methods for Getting— and Keeping—Customers

The term "guerilla marketing," coined by Jay Conrad Levinson in his book *Guerilla Marketing: How to Make Big Profits from Your Small Business* (Boston: Houghton Mifflin Co., 1985), is the best way I know to describe the kind of marketing and promotion that small, home-based businesses must do to survive and grow. Guerilla marketing consists of simple, creative, unique, resource-conservative, and effective efforts to get your name and work in front of the right prospects. I've collected quite a sampling of ideas—from my own experience and that of others—to share with you in this chapter.

No person with a knack for the communications business should be short on marketing ideas or the ability to implement them. What is important to remember, however, is the need to create a simple plan, focus on it, and follow through. An article entitled "The Practical Marketing Plan" by marketing consultant Adrienne Zoble in the January 1995 issue of *Home Office*

*Computing* drives home the point that, above all, it is important to keep your plan simple and straightforward.

Creating a marketing plan is an exercise that many small business owners avoid. They see it as an arduous task that will take up too much of their time and require a deep-pocket budget.

It's this fear that can stop your business dead in its track to success. As a marketing consultant, it's my job to defuse the myth of a marketing plan being a major project. I instead motivate entrepreneurs by explaining that it can be done in simple, workable increments, without taking significant time and money from your day-to-day operations. The steps are simple, and the rewards are numerous. Here's a story that illustrates how easy and successful a practical marketing plan can be.

A few years back, I held a small-business market planning seminar in Valley Forge, Pennsylvania. At the conclusion of the event, an insurance consultant from the audience took me aside and told me about his marketing budget. "It's $312 per year," he said. "Every week I take a client to lunch and we talk about his needs and my business. Problems? I address them quickly before they get out of hand. Good stuff? I use it on future sales calls. Referrals? I average two per luncheon and close deals on most of them. Each lunch runs about $30. The IRS lets me deduct 80 percent [remember, this was a few years ago] and that leaves me a cost of $6 times 52 weeks—a total of $312. What do you think, Adrienne?" I remarked, "If there were more businesspeople like you, I'd have to find a new line of work!"

I've told this story coast to coast to gales of laughter and feverish note taking. . . . And although the method for making my point is lighthearted, the logic is hard hitting. This entrepreneur has the perfect practical marketing plan because he works within his budgetary means, his method isn't time consuming, and he's learned how to reap big rewards from a simple tactic. You can do the same by implementing the following six steps to develop your own practical marketing plan.

1. *Diagnosis:* The purpose of the diagnosis is to determine where your business is and why. Take time to evaluate your position in the industry and in the eyes of your clients and prospects. Find out how you are perceived and systematically address any misconceptions. Ask yourself what image do your

letterhead, correspondence, and brochures convey? How do your promotional pieces and copy compare with those you receive in the mail? Although it's not necessary to spend lots of money on your printed materials, it is important to communicate professionalism, stability, and distinctiveness.

How is your sales follow-up? Do you market consistently? What services do you provide that your competitors don't (and vice versa)? Are customers requesting services that you resist offering because you already feel overwhelmed? How are sales and profitability compared with last year? Don't try to write any numbers down. You'll know off the top of your head if you're up, down, or flat. Now the difficult question: What factors are contributing to these circumstances? The answers to these questions will be the springboard for the next section.

2. *Prognosis:* Look at your answers to the questions in the diagnosis section. With them in mind, draw a conclusion about where'll you be a year from now if you continue on your present course.

3. *Goals and Objectives:* Set reasonable and measurable goals for where you want your business to be within six months to a year's time. For example, how many new clients do you want to acquire? Or how much in total revenue? *Don't try to plan for the long term or to concentrate on more than three goals, or you may begin to feel overwhelmed and discouraged* [emphasis added]. This would defeat the purpose of trying to develop this type of plan.

4. *Strategy:* The strategy and tactics sections will be the real nuts and bolts of your document. Concentrate on the things that you are equipped to do, not what you'd like to be able to do. Select two broad strategies for accomplishing your short-term goals and objectives. Let's take another look at the aforementioned insurance consultant. He employs two strategies: networking and follow-up. Although his methods are simple, he is successful because of his consistent, concentrated effort. You might want to focus on your public relations, repeat business, or telemarketing efforts. Emphasis, however, should not be placed on the number of strategies you choose but on how well you implement them.

Establish a marketing budget that falls between 2.5 percent and 7.5 percent of your gross sales (depending on profitability, amount of competition, stage of business growth, and need to educate your market). People and time are two other important factors to consider when creating a marketing budget. Be honest. It's not about what you want to do or what you think should be done—it's what you *can* do. Having unrealistic expectations can dishearten efforts and lead to stress.

5. *Tactics:* If you're going to embark on a direct-mail campaign, for example, you will need to determine who your recipients are, what you will send them, the products and services you want to highlight, the frequency of your mailings, follow-up activities, and how you will evaluate the results. Keep in mind that the number of mailings is not as important as the quality and continuity of your efforts. It's better, for example, to send six different mailings over the course of a year to 100 prospects and then follow up than it is to send a single message to 600 people followed by silence. Start by calling five people on the list for your current mailing each week.

6. *Analysis:* Implement your plan for at least three months. Then set aside time to look at which strategies were most and least effective. You might want to consider moving dollars from one strategy to another.

Don't be alarmed if you hit a roadblock while developing this type of plan. Step back, regroup, then start again—perhaps on a smaller scale. If you feel the task is still too burdensome, however, it might be worth your while to meet with a small business marketing consultant. A fresh professional eye might be able to hone your marketing plan or introduce some insights you've overlooked simply because you're too close to your business. Whether you do it alone or with the guidance of an independent professional, once you begin to spend time seriously thinking about your business, you'll wonder why you didn't develop this type of marketing plan sooner.

(Reprinted by permission from *Home Office Computing* magazine © 1995. For subscription information, call 800-288-7812.)

While I agree wholeheartedly with Ms. Zoble's entire article, I'd like to add one caveat for business start-ups in the area of budgeting. Set your budget based on how much revenue you *want*. If your worksheets in chapter 3 turned up a desired-annual-revenue figure of $100,000, then figure on spending

$2,500 to $7,500 to put your marketing plan into action. Keep that rule of thumb in place as the years go by and your business grows. If you spend only a percentage of what you currently make, you're likely to remain stagnant.

Now let's review the myriad ways you can flesh out this practical marketing plan with low-cost, effective marketing and promotional programs.

# Donate Your Skills

There are many ways to "spend" marketing dollars that don't involve mail list rental fees, postage, and printing costs. One way that was very successful for me when my business moved to a new community was to donate my time and skills for a community fundraising project.

At a neighborhood get-together shortly after we moved to Michigan from Connecticut, my husband and I prepared lobsters for our freshwater midwestern friends. A guest that evening noted my interest in cooking and my experience in writing and publishing and asked if I'd be interested in helping our community museum and historical society produce a cookbook. It seems the cookbook project had been attempted several times over a period of years, but it never got off the ground. My new friend, a well-known businesswoman in the community, seized on my writing, editing, and book production skills and asked me to join the cookbook committee. I readily agreed to help.

Over the next two years, I "gave" more than $5,000 worth of billable time in compiling, editing, and shepherding the cookbook through production and early marketing efforts. What I "got" far exceeds that number.

I met a dynamic group of women who were community leaders and doers. Many have become dear friends, especially Gail Kowalksi, through whose introduction I joined the committee, and Helen Lystra, the talented artist whose illustrations grace the cookbook cover and inside pages (and whose idea it was to produce it in the first place). As a result, I came to be a part of a wonderful community probably much sooner than I would have if I had turned down the project. Also, in researching the community's past (the cookbook had a historical-heritage theme) I learned much about my new home. And I got some great recipes to boot! These intangible benefits alone made the project worthwhile.

There have been tangible benefits, as well. The exposure and subsequent business referrals have more than reimbursed my time and efforts. I am working on communications projects for a wide range of local organizations as a result of referrals directly attributable to the contacts I made at the museum. (Thanks especially to the museum's education coordinator, Jeanne Willette, for that.)

Look around your own community. What business and other organizations might need your help with public relations, communications, and marketing? Is your community trying to foster the rebirth of its downtown area or to convert areas into green space? Is there a local bond issue up for a vote? Can you donate your skills to produce a brochure, a public service announcement, or a thirty-second television spot?

Get involved! Attend meetings and pay attention to determine who's running the show. Then make an appointment and offer your services in exchange for an acknowledgment of your company's contribution. Without being obvious, be sure to meet and greet the right people, and make sure they know about your contribution. Don't hide your light under a bushel basket. Promoter, promote thyself!

# Free Publicity

With any luck at all, your community activities will get noticed—and written about—in your local press. This happened for my business even before the cookbook was published. At another social gathering I met a reporter and we chatted about our common profession. She gave my name to another reporter, who contacted me to do a feature story on my business. I was interviewed and photographed; and having been a reporter myself and knowing something about being overworked and dealing with unbearable deadlines, I prepared a page or two of notes for the reporter as a courtesy so that she had correct spellings of names and places and a time line of events we discussed.

The story was published on the cover of the newspaper's weekly feature supplement on December 1, 1992. I'll never forget that day, because even before I read the article, the phone was ringing off its cradle. The exposure resulted in several thousand dollars' worth of work. A host of designers and writers got in touch, and I found the immensely talented and very computer-literate Adam Indyk, who now does the majority of Workwerks' graphic design, as a result of following up on those calls. Two years later, people still mention the article when we are introduced. The experience reminded me of my own repeated advice to clients over the years: "All publicity is good publicity."

## Create a Press Kit

Now, I didn't engineer that article so much as I seized upon an opportunity that came my way. But you can foster your own similar situation, particularly if your business is located in a small to medium-sized market with locally based newspapers and radio stations. Create your own press kit that emphasizes your company's unique services and deliver it to local media outlets. Follow up with telephone calls to editors, publishers, station managers, and the like. Offer to help with articles in your field or to be quoted as an "industry expert" on article topics with which you are familiar.

Another way to get an "in" with local media relates back to the previous section on donating services. Offer to handle the press releases and publicity for local nonprofit organizations. (I do it for St. Mary's School, which my son Matthew attends.) It helps develop a relationship with the media, and a camaraderie that is invaluable when you need to have a client's issues addressed. And it may help you get your own business publicized as well.

# Referrals

The majority of home-based-business owners responded to a survey about how they get work by saying that their chief marketing tool is word of mouth. Indeed, much of my success has been based on word of mouth. From the very beginning, clients who were pleased with my work gave my name to others.

Meeting other home-based professionals helped, too. Some of my best business has come my way as a result of referrals from other communications professionals who were themselves too busy to handle the clients. That's why you must stay out there, stay in touch, keep networking.

Contact the national organizations (for communications professionals that are listed in the Appendix) to learn if a local chapter is established near you. Most will allow you to attend at least one of their luncheon meetings for a modest fee without committing to costly annual membership. Attend a few meetings or networking sessions of various organizations to determine if potential business—or referral sources—exist. Along with other independent professionals like yourself, you'll meet corporate-communications people who might be potential clients or referral sources. If you choose to join, you can volunteer to help with membership mailings and newsletters, thus getting your name out even faster. All these things take time, however, so be sure to budget your commitments wisely.

Don't overlook the national organizations for home-based businesses listed in the Appendix. All have newsletters to which you can subscribe, and they may have chapters near you where you can meet with home-based-business owners engaged in a wide variety of pursuits. Through these meetings you may find referrals as well as support and camaraderie. You may also find other home-business owners and referrals at your local chapter of the National Association of Women Business Owners or through the networking organizations included in the Appendix.

Your local chamber of commerce should have a listing of business networks in your area, and your local chamber itself is also a good organization with which to start. By attending weekly or monthly breakfast meetings, you'll learn a lot about how business is conducted in your area and who conducts it. Then, of course, there are the original networking organizations found in virtually every community in the United States: the Rotary and the Jaycees.

The wonderful thing about operating a communications business is that it's a lot like operating an electric company or phone company—without the capital investment—because every business and organization must communicate. Very few do it as well as they could.

On a stroll down my hometown's main street during a lunch break, I encountered serious customer-service problems in our local branch of a statewide department store, an espresso bar that was dismally empty in the afternoon (even though shoppers were out in force and two newspaper offices and several banks are located within a block of it), and many other businesses that could boost traffic by applying creative communications and marketing techniques. And if I hadn't been under the gun to finish this book, I would have probably set about making some phone calls and writing a proposal letter when I returned to the office.

I've often wondered how much more money even successful businesses could make if they would just communicate properly—and regularly. Look around your own community. You'll probably find dozens of businesses that need your help—badly. Your mission, should you choose to accept it, is to convince them of the need for your services.

## Fostering Referrals by Current Clients

Your clients may not need any prodding to refer you to others. The referrals may be automatic. When that happens, I urge you to express your appreciation just as automatically, always with a letter of thanks. I also like to send small gifts, such as gift baskets of goodies, flowers, a framed photograph.

IRS rules limit the tax deductibility of gifts to clients to $25 per client per gift. That often doesn't give you a lot of room to make your thanks commensurate to the good deed done you, particularly if there's a large project—and fee—involved. You can choose to send a larger gift and not write off the remainder, or you can remember your clients throughout the year—at birthdays, Christmas, the birth of a child, business anniversaries, and other times. I like to take clients to lunch, and throughout the year at various times to send flowers or custom gift baskets filled with thoughtful gifts and goodies, prepared by another home-based-business owner I know: Terrie Lusis of New England Presence, 297 Plains Road, Haddam, CT 06438 (203) 345–2859 (telephone or fax). Write or call for a catalog chock-full of reasonably priced and beautifully presented baskets of edibles and other goodies for every occasion. There are lots of home-based gift basket businesses in operation. Terrie's is the best I've ever seen.

If you'd like to step up the pace of referrals, you can try more overt tactics. In the November 1993 issue of *Home Office Computing,* an article entitled "Make Word of Mouth Work" by Donna Partow offered many suggestions. Here are some excerpts.

Rather than waiting passively for word of mouth to work its magic, why not give people something to talk about? All you need is an effective referral program. . . .

But before you jump into your own program, be aware that referral incentives may not always create a win-win situation. They can backfire if you overstep professional boundaries or put any pressure on your existing customers to send new business to you. An incentive program tends to work best when you never directly ask people to sell for you. Instead . . . just lay the idea of referral incentives before your customers. If they want to pick up the ball and run with it, fine. Otherwise, let go of the idea. Don't push it.

The referral program you develop will depend on several factors, including the nature of your business, who your customers are, and how urgently you need new business. Outlined . . . are three key elements: education, inspiration, and communication.

### Educate Your Customers

Assuming you offer high-quality products or services, *your existing customers represent your best source of future business* [emphasis added]. They've experienced the benefits of working with you, so their recommendations carry more weight than a dozen direct-mail campaigns and 10 cold calls combined.

Yet many of your customers probably think you have all the business you need. Others may not realize the full range of products and services you offer. Your circle of influence—family, friends, and former or current colleagues—represents another often-untapped source of referrals. Even if these people don't need your product or service, they undoubtedly know others who do. However, they can't refer customers to you if they don't understand your business.

One easy-to-use educational tool is a capabilities brochure, which presents an overview of your business. After reading your brochure, customers and everyone else in your circle of influence should be able to describe what you do, who needs your products or services, what qualifies you to perform the service or provide the product, and what sets you apart from the competition, how long you've been in business, and any noteworthy achievements or customers served.

In addition, include a section in the brochure (or prepare a separate flier) describing your referral-incentive program. It should clarify when—under what circumstances—people should refer someone to your business, what procedures they should follow when referring, and how and when you will reward them for referring customers to you. The essential types of rewards include future discounts, free products or services, a referral fee, and gifts. . . .

### Inspire Your Customers

A few kind souls will refer customers to you just for the sheer joy of helping others. And a few other business owners will provide referrals in the hope that you'll help them in return. Whatever the reason, though, a little inspiration always helps. So states Diana Booher, corporate trainer and prolific author of 26 books on business communications.

"Whenever we do a corporate program, we ask the customer to write a testimonial letter," says Booher, who recently moved Booher Consultants out of her Euless, Texas, home when her staff grew to 12. "We ask the customer to document any positive comments and to address specific issues like why they decided to hire us and what the results were."

These inspirational letters achieve three objectives. First, writing an endorsement of your business strengthens the customer's commitment to you. They now have a vested interest in your success. Second, they understand you are in the market for new customers and may immediately refer someone. And third, you have ammunition when seeking new accounts.

Once Booher receives the letter, she sends the customer a gift, such as an autographed book or a cassette tape series. "Customers are always thrilled because it's so unexpected," she says. "Often they'll call to say, 'I've never received anything like this before; no one ever went to the trouble.'" The next time they hear of someone needing a trainer, whom do you think they recommend?

"Even if the referral doesn't become a paying customer until three years later, we still pay the promised fee," stresses Booher. Such honesty goes a long way toward inspiring future referrals.

### Remind Your Customers

Your efforts to educate and inspire your customers will not be complete without the final component: communication. That's spelled "f-r-e-q-u-e-n-t r-e-m-i-n-d-e-r-s," but it's only the icing on the incentive cake you've already baked.

(Reprinted by permission from *Home Office Computing* magazine © 1995. For subscription information, call 800-288-7812.)

One of the "frequent reminders" you might send to clients is a letter or mini-flier with a gift certificate for services—$100 worth, for example—and the words "Deduct $100 from your next invoice when you refer another business to [your business name]."

Your business card can double as a referral reminder as well. On the back of it have printed a referral incentive, such as "Refer an associate to [name] and receive $100 [or 10 percent] off your next invoice."

Whatever referral reminders you choose—be they letters, brochures, gift certificates, fliers, or specially printed business cards—your objective is to keep clients continually aware that you encourage and reward referrals. In addition, you must track all referrals to make sure the appropriate, promised rewards are delivered promptly. Clients must also know that those they refer to you will receive consistent, high-quality service and timely turnaround. Your integrity and the quality of your work are your best advertisements for continuing referrals.

## Advertising Specialty Items

A fairly inexpensive way to say "thank you" for a referral (or for a client's business in general) that doubles as a reminder about your business is through advertising specialty items imprinted with your logo and phone number. Advertising specialty companies and catalogs abound. (You'll start to receive solicitations from these companies the minute you register your business at your city hall or county office building or put your business name on other mailing lists. ) You can have your name, phone number, and a motivational message printed on coffee mugs, calendars, rulers, note pads, memo cubes, Post-it notes, refrigerator (or file cabinet) magnets, and so on.

## Build Your Mailing List

No amount of gifts, geegaws, and referral incentives will work unless you communicate regularly with your past and existing customers, with those who can potentially refer new customers, and with prospective customers themselves. Accordingly, you need to build—and continually update and "clean up"—your own computerized mailing list.

Anyone you meet on a sales call or who phones should be asked for telephone numbers and mailing address. People you meet at organization lunches and other get-togethers who strike you as potential clients or referral sources should also be added to your list. Ask for a business card, and key your entries accordingly: current clients, past clients, prospects, referral sources, suppliers, other communications professionals, and the like.

## Your Own Newsletter

Send mailings from time to time (see the next section, on sales letters) or even create your own regular newsletter to mail to your list. In it offer helpful information on communication techniques, statistics on marketing, and feature articles and photos about communications successes you've had with your own clients (with client permission, of course). If time permits, attach a handwritten or typed personal note with each newsletter. If not, make sure the most vital clients and prospects get individual attention.

## Super Sales Letters

Since you're in the marketing and communications field, you shouldn't have any trouble creating sales letters that work. You know the rules: snappy opener ("the hook"), bulleted lists, short paragraphs, white space, emphasis on benefits to the customer, and so forth. With desktop publishing, you can pull out the stops with clip art, scanned-in photos, and other eye-catching graphics. But no amount of clever copy and great graphics will help unless the letter is *specific to the customer.* Know your audience. Don't be glib and clever unless the client will respond to that approach. See the accompanying box for an example.

# WORDWERKS
## A Communications Company

April 3, 1995

Mr. Boris Bigwig
Bigwig Business, Inc.
1000 Industrial Way
Anytown, USA

Dear Mr. Bigwig:
You know that your business must communicate to survive and grow.

> Current and prospective customers,
> employees,
> suppliers,
> distributors,
> manufacturers' representatives

. . . all these "constituents " play a vital role in your business success. They need regular, up-to-date information from you.

But who has time to design brochures, product fact sheets, newsletters, and catalogs; hire photographers and illustrators; get the best quotes from printers; build and maintain mailing lists; and follow up, follow up, follow up?

We do!

We're **Wordwerks Communications**, a locally owned and operated business staffed by experienced communications professionals. Our experience and expertise in quality communication products that boost your bottom line—*without breaking your budget*—will free you to do what you do best: run your business.

I think you'll like our ideas. I know you'll like our efficiency and reasonable prices. Our free, no obligation, communications consultation will point out ways you can communicate more effectively *and* cost-effectively. I'll call you next week to set up a time when we can spend an hour together discussing your communication needs.

Sincerely,
WORDWERKS


Louann N. Werksma
Director

**Sample Sales Letter**

## Follow Up, Follow Up, Follow Up

The letter, once read, gets your foot in the door and gives your name a familiar "ring" when you follow up. Do follow up—with a telephoned invitation to meet over lunch or at the client's office to discuss the client's communications needs.

Don't give up. If you sense interest, make three sincere attempts to secure an appointment before you put the prospect on the back burner. If the client is too preoccupied with other activities at the time you've made initial contact, drop a note in your tickler file to call in a month or two. Eventually you'll know instinctively when a prospect is only stringing you along because he or she cannot bear to let you down with a firm "no interest" reply.

# Selling Yourself Successfully

Remember, whatever marketing you choose to do, make it a part of a concerted, practical, doable *plan*. Once you have a good plan in place, fund it properly and allot time to carry it out. Set aside one day a week—or every other week—to cast your line for future business and you won't get caught in the self-employment syndrome known as the feast-and-famine cycle. You'll have the business you want when you want it.

## Silver and Gold

When I think of getting—and keeping—clients, I think of a simple tune I sang as a Girl Scout way too many years ago: "Make new friends, but keep the old/One is silver and the other gold." Established client relationships are golden. Polish them till they gleam with goodwill. Be there when established clients call, give them your best efforts, and avoid the temptation to shirk them for the shine of a new client romance. Every year, when I look at my revenue totals per client, it's plain to me where my bread is buttered. The clients who have been with me since the beginning, who've waited patiently and adjusted schedules for my vacations and two maternity leaves, who have cut checks early or in advance to smooth out my cash flow crises, and who keep relying on me for their communications needs are the relationships I treasure the most.

In chapter 7 several Wordwerks clients get a turn to talk about what it's like to do business with a home-based communications professional. Appropriately, the chapter begins with my fourteen-karat-gold, eight-year relationship with Pivot Point International, Inc., of Chicago and its executive vice president, Gordon Miller.

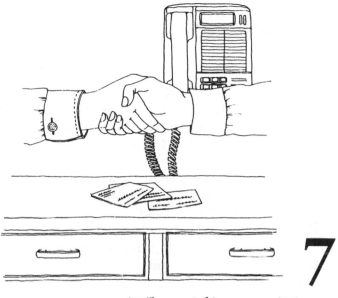

# 7

# The Clients' Turn
## Perspectives on Hiring a Home-Based Communications Professional

## An Interview with Gordon Miller

Gordon Miller and I met one cold January day in 1986 in Salt Lake City. He was the director of operations for a chain of twelve cosmetology schools. I was the director of educational services for a publishing company that had sold him a business-management education package for his schools. I flew out from Connecticut to conduct an in-service seminar for his instructors, to help them teach such subjects as business math, business laws, and small-business marketing to their students, many of whom would one day open their own hair salons.

Gordon and I connected immediately. He had a degree in finance and a mind that was keenly logical at the same time that it was creative. Through unexpected circumstances (how many of us don't find our careers "by accident?"), he had become involved in, and eventually a recognized expert on, government financial aid for higher education. That led to positions as a financial-aid officer at large cosmetology school operations, to a stint as a consultant to cosmetology schools, and to the director-of-operations position where I first met him.

Impressed by his expertise on a wide range of educational-management subjects and his insights into industry issues, I hired Gordon as a speaker for school management seminars I was conducting around the country later that year. At one of those seminars, executives from Pivot Point International, Inc., a leading publisher of cosmetology education programs, heard Gordon speak and offered him a marketing position at Pivot Point's world headquarters in Chicago. He accepted and in the ensuing years was promoted up the management ladder to executive vice president.

About the time Gordon went to work for Pivot Point, I founded Wordwerks. In early 1987, he began producing *Focus,* a management newsletter for schools that were teaching Pivot Point's educational programs. His in-house staff was already taxed to the limit with existing communication and marketing projects. Rather than hire more staff, he contracted Wordwerks, and thus began our association as client and supplier.

Over the years, Wordwerks has written and produced four different newsletters for various Pivot Point customer groups, developed a communications textbook and instructor manual, written training videos, and produced seminar manuals, brochures, and a wide range of other collateral materials. Although our face-to-face meetings have sometimes been years apart, Gordon and I communicate at least weekly (and often daily) by phone, fax, and CompuServe.

At times I have been tempted to take for granted my relationship with Gordon Miller and Pivot Point. After all, they've always been a client. At times in the past, they've been Wordwerks' *only* active client. But when I generate quarterly and annual statements of income, Pivot Point is consistently one of Wordwerks' "top" clients in terms of revenue. And always a top client in terms of mutual respect and an excellent working relationship.

Based on that glowing review of our relationship, you might

expect my interview with Gordon Miller to have been a page from the handbook of the mutual admiration society. But he, like other clients when asked for their candid reviews of our working relationship, made suggestions that made me sit up and take notice. I hope you will do the same.

Q. How would you compare your experiences hiring a home-based communications company with hiring full-service agencies or in-house staff? Specifically, discuss your experience in terms of cost, turnaround time, ease of communicating needs and having them met, access, and quality of work.

A. I've worked with all three—in-house creative departments, large agencies, and small companies like Wordwerks—and dollar-wise, I come out better with outsourcing. Although even a small company like yours bills me at more than twice the hourly rate I pay in-house staff, I don't have the risk, nor do I have to pay unemployment insurance and benefits. We're a company that "self-insures," and we assume the first $50,000 of medical payments for our employees, so that's an overhead item I don't have with freelancers and outside companies.

Outsourcing to companies such as Wordwerks helps me overcome the inefficiencies inherent in a small corporate structure. I pay my creative employees for forty hours whether they are producing or out sick or sitting in meetings, plus there is the cost of direct management. I avoid the training cost and learning curve of hiring people, as well. When you hire an outside person or agency, you expect them to be up to speed and not charge you excessively for nonproductive time. It's also a lot easier to get rid of them if you don't like their work.

When we're running a seminar or symposium or producing a new textbook package, we get into a real crunch, and outsourcing helps us meet that temporary workload without bringing on extra staff.

Another benefit with freelancers and independent agencies is *artistic diversity*. You can get a fresh approach to the look and feel of a marketing piece; . . . sometimes in-house people get hooked on one type style or design.

All in all, I've been generally happy with our working relationship. . . .

**Q. Generally? Do I hear a "but" coming?**

A. Well, sure, nobody's perfect. The big difference with outside services is that I have no control over their priorities. Sometimes I need immediate attention, and you're not there when I call so I have to wait. You know there have been times when we've played phone tag for days. That can get frustrating.

Also, when you're "on the clock" with a supplier you're sensitive to their time. You're tempted to compromise if something isn't quite right. Either way, you pay for it in the end. Through experience, I've found it's worth it to spend the extra money and time to rework something to get it right.

In the final analysis, we probably spend the same amount of money on outsourced communications as we do on those produced in-house. The real benefit comes from having the extra capacity "on call" and on the quality of the finished product and the turnaround. You provide value in the quality of work that you do and in your built-in knowledge of my industry and customers. I've been lucky to work with you.

Now, let's talk about the premiere issue of our new customer publication. . . .

# An Interview with Tim Breed

I was introduced to, and subsequently hired by, Tim Breed through a designer with whom we both worked, Sheila Warners of Sheila Warners Design. In his role as the manager of community relations for Hackley Hospital in Muskegon, Michigan, Tim hired Wordwerks to provide writing and editing services on

*To Your Health,* the hospital's quarterly community newsletter, which Sheila Warners had been designing for some time. Of all my clients, Tim is one of the easiest to work with, inasmuch as he once did what I do. As a matter of fact, in addition to having been a freelance writer and designer of publications and marketing materials, he once worked as an on-air radio personality, so he knows the ins and outs of the communications profession far better than do most people who contract for this type of work.

In the course of running the busy community relations department of a community hospital with a tremendous public outreach philosophy, overseeing many corporate partnerships for wellness programs in the community, and shepherding a diverse catalog of publications through production, he still on occasion rolls up his sleeves to write and design some of the hospital's PR material. I knew he would have unique insights to share with readers of this book.

Q. How would you compare your experiences hiring a home-based communications company with hiring full-service agencies or in-house staff? Specifically, discuss your experience in terms of cost, turnaround time, ease of communicating needs and having them met, access, and quality of work.

A. I don't think there is that much difference between the work of a full-service agency and a home-based business. Even in large agencies, you're usually assigned to one individual who coordinates your project and handles all communication, so you develop a relationship similar to that of working with a one-person shop.

I usually bring a vision of what I want to the table, no matter who I am working with. Knowing what I want in advance, I stay closely involved throughout production.

Now cost is another matter. Without exception, the cost is much less when you hire a home-based business. In my experience, there's no question about that. Working with in-house people, I have payroll and benefit expenses I don't have with agencies or freelance workers, so I think price is probably better with the home-based business versus the in-house staff as well.

The advantage of doing a project in house is that the work is never out of sight. You can keep an eye on it and tweak it to be what you want. Of course, on the flip side of that, organizations develop their own "language" or vocabulary that they understand perfectly well. On occasion, they forget that their outside audiences don't know what they're talking about. A freelance writer coming into that situation can be helpful. His or her objectivity helps translate the language for an outside audience to understand.

Q. Now I have a question that might be difficult to answer, but I appreciate your candor and your advice. When we first started working together, I was so immediately caught up in the friendly atmosphere and openness of your organization that, looking back, I realize that I probably overstepped a fine line that outsiders walk. Although there is a great team spirit and camaraderie going on in some of our client organizations, we have to remember that we are, after all, outsiders. How would you advise home-based business owners on that score?

A. You're right, that is a difficult question. I guess I can go back to my own experience. I had one client that was all spit and polish, friendly on the surface, but that client made it clear that friendliness and friendship were two different things. For your readers who will be working outside their own communities, I would just caution them that different locales have different attitudes and values.

I know what incident you are referring to. You felt that you had overstepped your bounds as a contract employee and got involved in some interviews that I didn't request and sort of took the article beyond where I wanted it to go . . . . It's not always easy at first to figure out a corporate culture and the subtle codes and rules that insiders instinctively know.

My comment to you and your readers would be, with any new client, I would believe you'd find it beneficial to schedule a series of meetings close together at the outset. These "fact-finding" meetings will help you pick up on clues and learn how the chain of authority in an organization works.

And I'd also urge you not to take any perceived coolness personally. There are times when you bring an outsider in and you're working on a project pretty closely over a period of time. You have lunch together, the contractor is part of the team for a while. When the project is over, the emphasis reverts back to the in-house "family," so to speak.

From the contractor's perspective, there's a double-edged sword. On the one hand, it's great to be part of a team again and get in on all the camaraderie. On the other hand, the diversity [freelancing offers] is a real benefit. It gives you an opportunity to interact with different people. It's very thought-provoking and mind-opening to move in and out of different organizations conducting different kinds of businesses.

Q. I agree. Thank you for addressing that issue. I wanted the readers of my book, many of whom will be fresh from corporations and institutions, to understand the different role they will now play.

I have one last question. What advice would you give to outside agencies as to how much client contact is enough versus how much is too much? In other words, how often should a supplier call on a client when there is no project going on at the time?

A. I personally prefer the occasional contact. I think once a month is a good interval. It reminds me that there is someone there who is interested in working with us. I don't view it negatively at all. In fact, sometimes I need a gentle prodding to remind me that it's time to get working on a certain project. I'm pulled in so many directions in my daily work that occasionally suppliers have to wave a flag to get my attention. Therefore, I appreciate the occasional "Hi there! Do you know what month this is?" message.

When there's a project in progress, then a call once or

twice a week to update me on progress is certainly within reason.

Q. Now that you mention it, Tim . . .

# An Interview with Rich Nemesi

Rich Nemesi is a marketing executive for a Fortune 500 computer product and service company. We agreed that we wouldn't use his company's name in order to avoid the lengthy approval process that would have been necessary. A fairly recent client, Rich's department contracted with Wordwerks to produce a regional customer publication focusing on customer successes with the company's products and services. For Wordwerks, it was a first in terms of the type of client. We'd never worked with a multibillion-dollar-a-year, multinational public corporation before. But we were very familiar with the subject and scope of the particular project (which continued to grow and expand weekly); and we were more than eager to accept the challenge it presented. After all, what a feather in our portfolio to have *this* company's logo on materials we had produced!

Since Rich is busy supervising a large marketing force and doing all the things corporate executives do, he and I stay in touch via occasional updates. In other words, I find my way around his organization and get our publication out without bugging him too much. I wondered how he thought our working relationship was working out, so I posed the same questions to him.

Q. How would you compare your experiences hiring a home-based communications company with hiring full-service agencies or in-house staff? Specifically, discuss your experience in terms of cost, turnaround time, ease of communicating needs and having them met, access, and quality of work.

A. For our area, the cost is lower but still comparable. The turnaround, as well, is comparable. The quality of work is better. Your value is that you're more creative. You bring a diverse background to your work, and that gave us a fresh look and feel for our publication. It has been very well received.

One of my staff was pleasantly surprised when our first issue came out. He called to say, "I wasn't sure what we'd get from a woman working in an office over her garage, but this is a great publication." I think you proved your professional integrity and creativity early on.

Q. Thank you. What suggestions would you have for aspiring home-based business owners who want to promote their services to, and work effectively with, a large corporation?

The key is in communications. We're all becoming more home-based. Many of my staff work from their homes, their cars, the customers' locations. Work has changed, and I think even bastions of business like my company are more accepting of "nontraditional" work modes.

But I think you have to make yourself as accessible as possible, and maybe even hide the fact that you're one person. I need to know that, if you get hit by a car tomorrow, someone will fill your shoes and be able to produce as good a product as you can, without my getting involved.

Your value is that you deliver a one-on-one service that is unique. Your competitive edge comes from your knowledge and skill. But perhaps you need to look into business support and backup services that make you more responsive to your clients. Consider a live answering service or a pager. When I call and get a recording and I can't hit the "zero" and "pound" keys and get transferred to a receptionist who knows something about me and our business, I get worried.

Also, consider getting an Internet address. Fax machines are great, but my main business tools are my car, my cellular phone, and my notebook computer. At times, I haven't been in my office to receive faxes when you've sent them. If you could send articles to me by e-mail, I could respond much more quickly from wherever I happened to be. You could put your e-mail address right on your stationery, and it would show customers one more way you make yourself accessible to them.

When you deal with Fortune 500 companies, that always makes a mark. It's a minor detail, but it could be critical, and therefore you should plan for contingencies.

We're all outsourcing our noncritical business activities. Compared with three years ago, we're conducting business very differently today. We're focusing on the technology and services we deliver, and finding better, more efficient ways to do business.

You've brought us a fresh approach to communicating with our clients, and we hope to keep using your skills even as we continue to transform our business to meet the demands of a fiercely competitive environment.

## Solutions for a New Era

Whew! I asked for honesty, and I got what I asked for. Because I was so busy with client projects, I equated "busy" with "client satisfaction." In fact, I learned I wasn't always meeting my clients' needs.

After these client interviews, I made some calls to business consultants to learn how I could upgrade my equipment and business practices to be more accessible and responsive to customers. And I did some soul searching on the very nature of working as a home-based communications company.

The results can be found in the next chapter, "Growing Your Business." As I said earlier, standing still is going backwards. We must all adapt to change, or time and opportunity will pass us by. So before I leave you to contemplate starting a home-based business, I offer one final chapter on how to move on from there.

# 8

# Growing Your Business
## Thoughts about What to Do
## After You Achieve Success

"How many of you, if you won the lottery tonight, would still get up tomorrow morning and go to work?"

That question was posed to a group of small-business owners by the guest speaker at a meeting of the Michigan Association of Women Entrepreneurs. It took a roomful of decisive go-getters by surprise. No one responded for a time, but eventually about one-fourth of the women in the audience raised a hand. It took a while, but I raised mine.

The speaker, a noted author and lecturer, went on to highlight her five points for continued small-business success. I took notes, but my mind kept wandering back to her first question.

Why did I have to think about my answer? I love my work. I have always wanted to be a writer. At the age of ten, with a manual typewriter given to me as a Christmas present, I published my first newsletter. If someone would have told me back then that I'd actually make a decent living doing what I loved best, I would have thought nothing could be better.

Furthermore, I wanted to be self-employed and work at home the minute I knew I was to be a mother. I love the freedom to schedule both personal and professional time, the diverse and often surprising nature of the work, the fact that with every ring of the phone there is a potential new adventure. So what made me hesitate before raising my hand?

*Burnout.*

Simple as that. Thinking that I could do it all and do it well. Based on the percentage of hands that went up in that room, I wasn't the only one suffering from it. This was, after all, a roomful of successful women business owners. We are considered to be living the American Dream.

And the majority of us, I am sure, had read books and attended seminars on time management and business practices to help us organize, set priorities, and take it one step at a time. From my conversations with women (and men) I've met at these and similar meetings, I've concluded that there's no shortage of brains, ambition, and skill among us. We know what it takes to be successful. Any one of the business owners I know could write the "textbook" on how to run a business.

But, just as we "know" intellectually what it takes to be healthy, for example, what foods to eat and how much exercise to get, we don't all follow the prescription. Life intervenes, and we get carried away with tasks, worries, and demands. We assign false importance to what we do and make unreasonable demands of ourselves. My father, a very wise man, once said to me, "You can get the best job in the world, the job you always wanted, and find yourself one day walking away from it in frustration. You just get yourself too caught up."

*Perspective.* My father, I now realize, was telling me to maintain my perspective.

In the midst of my reverie that evening, I managed to hear the speaker ask another question: "When was the last time any of you took out your business plan and looked at it? Much less revised it?"

From the guilty twitter that spread across the room, anyone could guess the answer. There's not a business management volume written, this one included, that doesn't offer advice and tips on writing that first necessary business plan. About half the small-business owners I know have actually put the time into writing one. The majority, once their plans have been written and served their intended purpose (usually to secure financing), file them away. "Planning" thereafter is something forced upon them by a problem that demands a solution or a situation that requires attention. Such was the situation I found myself in that night.

I was overwhelmed by my business at that moment. I had a greater quantity and quality of work than I had ever expected. But I was working seven days a week, and deadlines were slipping. I was outsourcing everything I could (or so I thought), but it seemed, to paraphrase the Pennsylvania Dutch, "the hurrier I went, the behinder I got." All my systems for work and time management were breaking down as file after file of partially finished projects covered all work surfaces in my office. To top it all off, the manuscript for this book was overdue on my long-suffering editor's desk by nearly six months.

The speaker went on to advise us all to take a day and get away from our offices. To take our employees with us and to go somewhere far from the phones and dream about what our businesses could be.

I took her advice. I escaped from a cold West Michigan winter to the shores of a blue Pacific bay for two days. I thought about me, my work, my home-based business. And I dreamed. The results turned into this, a final chapter about maintaining your passion for work at the same time you keep your perspective, about planning and setting priorities, and about getting the help you need to get the job done.

For you *will* be successful. Of that I am certain. It's always been my belief that, in America, it's easy to make money. What's not so easy is to find lasting happiness. I'd be willing to bet we have far fewer happy people than we have rich people. And what good is being rich, or successful, or having a reputation for being the best at what you do, if you can't enjoy your success and be happy?

Here are my pointers for building "safeguards for happiness" into your new home-based business, as revealed to me by a muse who materialized through the sunshine and blue skies during my reverie by the bay.

# Planning as a Process

Life is a journey, not a destination," said Confucius.

The same can be said for business. You don't buy or start a business and then have a static thing. It keeps moving. You move with it. So, build into your business a philosophy that recognizes planning as a *process* rather than as a task that, once done, can be left behind.

Take your brand-spanking-new desk calendar out right now and block off one day each quarter for the next year. Write in the words "Planning Day." Don't make appointments for that day. Don't stay in the office listening to your phone mail messages as they pile up. Go away with your business records and evaluate where you've been in the three months since you last updated your plan and where you want to go from there. List one or two short-term goals, and the required steps for achieving them. Set goals and priorities in the areas of business management, marketing, and professional growth.

# Focus on Excellence and Get Good Advice

In the beginning, you'll probably take on work just because you need the money. Eventually, you'll come to find out what it is you do best. Continually evaluate and reevaluate what you do best, and concentrate on developing your specialty.

It's also important to locate and invest in good people to help you run your business. I'm not necessarily talking about full-time employees, but consultants and others who can help free you to focus on your clients and your finished product.

If you do hire full-time employees, don't fall into the trap of hiring neighbors, relatives, or friends just because they happen to be handy or need a job. According to "the experts," that's one of the small-business owner's most fatal pitfalls. Because a small business relies on fewer people, each person has to be truly expert at what he or she does. If you find the right people to work with you, finding a way to pay them won't be a problem.

Here's my new and expanded list of consultants and contractors who make up my support team.

- Freelance writers (for backup when I get overbooked)
- Photographers
- Graphic designers and illustrators
- A computer consultant to help me maintain and upgrade my computing capability
- A telephone consultant to help me maintain and upgrade my telephone equipment and services to meet the needs of my growing business
- A bookkeeping service to handle my monthly and quarterly statements and government filings (well worth the cost in terms of freeing up my time to do what I do best)
- A new proofreader to whom I delegate responsibility for making sure the finished product is correct, and who doubles as a production assistant handling the back-and-forth of proof between my freelance designers, the printer, and my office

Advice is all around you. A good place to start is your local Small Business Development Office of the Small Business Administration. The Service Corps of Retired Executives (SCORE) is another offshoot of the SBA that can be a rich resource for your budding business. These retired volunteers can help you fill in the gaps in your business-management expertise. All of these offices can be found in your telephone book under "United States Government."

## Find Temporary Help

As for support people, if you're not ready to hire full-time staff, look into temporary staffing services in your area. Get to know what they offer before you need them, so that when you need to bridge the gap between the number of hours of work you have left to do and the number of hours remaining in the day, you'll know where to go for the right help.

College and university internship programs are another excellent source of low-cost (sometimes free) temporary help. Contact any institutions in your area that have business and communications programs and inquire about their student intern programs. Set up these relationships now, before you need them.

## Maintain Your Perspective

When you have a day like the one I described in the introduction, a day when all the forces of the universe seem to be conspiring against you, don't get your britches in a knot. Keep your perspective. Remember, you provide a vital service and you are a respected professional; but you are not saving lives or curing world hunger. This is, after all, work. And work is an important part of life, but not life itself.

F. Scott Fitzgerald, through his main character in the short story *Babylon Revisited,* said that there were only two reasons to get up in the morning: work to do and someone to love. If you have both, rejoice. Never sacrifice the latter for the former.

## Take Care of Yourself

In chapter 7, you might remember, one of my clients raised a thought-provoking issue. He essentially asked me, What would I do if you got hit by a car tomorrow? How would I know my publication would get finished?

While my client's hypothetical question may appear, on the surface, unsympathetic, his motives were easy for me to understand. He is, after all, a practical business person. Why should he hire me if I haven't planned for such contingencies?

In the past, my contingency planning focused on *my* needs: disability insurance to pay the bills in case I become incapacitated, for example. I hadn't even considered the repercussions to my clients if I become unable to finish their projects. The fact that two pregnancies and the devastating, unexpected deaths of both my parents in a six-week period hadn't kept me from completing a project in the past was no guarantee that something couldn't happen in the future to prevent me from fulfilling my business commitments.

Of all the topics I considered during my two-day planning retreat, this one really gave me pause. If I were my clients, I too would want to hire a company that could come through notwithstanding fire, flood, or act of God. Creative skills and cost-effectiveness are important competitive advantages, to be sure, but they are not everything. I realized I would need to plan more completely for such contingencies.

One of the obvious ways to avoid not being there for clients or loved ones is to take care of yourself. There are twenty-four hours in a day. You give at least eight to your clients and probably that many to your family, I told myself. The least you can do is to promise to give one to yourself. One hour a day. An hour to relax, read a book, take an exercise class, go for a walk, sit by the river. All by myself.

Try it. It is amazing how many problems seem to work themselves out once you are rested and refreshed. Along with practicing what you know to be a healthy lifestyle, give yourself a minimum one-hour break each and every day. (Lunch hour doesn't count. I know you read the mail or run errands or talk on the phone.) One hour a day. Seven days a week. Not for your spouse, your kids, your friends, your church, your charities, or your work. For you.

That said, my client's question still haunted me. I had gotten by for nearly nine years "doing it all" myself. But now I had come to realize that my success had gotten the better of me. I was on the verge of a decision.

# Know When It's Time to Grow

After nine years as a self-described "solo home-based communications professional," I can feel a change in the wind. The youngest of our three sons is registered for kindergarten. In another year or so he'll be in school full-time. The oldest is now a teenager. So many interesting projects beckon, and I'm beginning to sense that the freedom to pursue them is coming.

## Space Considerations

When you arrive at the decision to "grow" your business, consider the available options. You may not need to move out of your home office. Space might allow you to work with others right where you are. Consider, however, what impact that might have upon your coworkers and employees. It's not easy to work in the presence of another person's family members going about their personal lives.

But you're not limited to renting expensive corporate offices if you do decide you've outgrown your home-based space. Look into the availability of state- and community-sponsored "business incubators." These are physical facilities that provide office space and, often, secretarial and other office support. Your local and state chambers of commerce and/or economic development offices can help you locate business incubator facilities near you.

If no publicly sponsored business incubator space exists in your area, there are many private businesses that offer similar features and benefits. For a reasonable monthly fee, you'll get an office in a building staffed by a receptionist, and possibly other shared services and equipment as well.

Most of these businesses offer conference and meeting rooms you can schedule in advance. In addition, you can forward your phones to the receptionist, which gives you the benefit of a "warm" response to your clients' calls. Unlike an answering service, this arrangement can prove very effective because the receptionist often gets to know something about you and your business and can therefore be more helpful to clients than a distant answering service can. Usually, you'll find copy machines and secretarial services available a la carte. Moving to a shared facility can be a sound and cost-effective next step, one that allows you to evaluate how well you like being "out of the house" and how it affects your business and your life.

## Planning for Contingencies

I am considering several options for developing my business into one that won't flounder if something happens to its owner. One is to work with a partner—an idea I rejected in the past. There are several people I know now whom I would trust as partners and whose expertise would complement mine and add value for clients.

Another option, should a partnership not materialize, is to become more involved with fellow professionals who provide occasional backup (see the section in chapter 5 entitled "The Virtual Agency"). They could take over and complete a project if I were unable to do so.

## A New Focus

Still another solution is to focus your business on products and services that are not "time-dependent." As I wrote earlier in this book, when you provide a service and bill by the hour, you will always be limited by the number of hours you have to work and the rate you can charge. By developing communications "products," such as survey packages, ready-made newsletters for specific markets, scripted training programs, communications seminars, and other similar "inventions" you are able to copyright and sell to more than one client, you transform your business from a professional-service company based on the skills of specific individuals to a marketing organization with an entire line of products to sell.

I haven't decided exactly what is in the future for Wordwerks and me. I am, however, taking my own advice and doing the necessary nitty-gritty planning and preparation that will lead me to the right decision.

Accordingly, watch for the sequel to this book, tentatively titled *How to Expand and Develop Your Marketing and Communications Company.* No publication date has been set. (And no editor willing to deal with this writer has yet committed to the project.)

Meanwhile, you have my best wishes for your success as you open and operate your home-based communications company. I envy you all the new experiences that await you: the exhilaration you'll feel on that first morning, when you enter your newly set-up office with a cup of steaming coffee in hand, ready to make your company everything you want it to be; the excitement when that first client says yes to your proposal; the satisfaction in work well done when the first communications piece you produce arrives fresh from the printer (sans errors!); the thrill of that first check in the mailbox with all those zeros in it (followed by the rueful realization that only part of it is yours to spend after you write checks of your own against it); the joy of juggling several different projects at once, competently and well.

As for me, there are still a few "firsts" to anticipate with excitement. Right now, I'm looking forward to the first time a box arrives on my doorstep containing freshly minted books that have *my* name on the cover. Life—and work—are good.

# Appendix

## Recommended Reading

### Books

Applegate, Jane. *Succeeding in Small Business: The 101 Toughest Problems and How to Solve Them*. New York: Plume/Penguin Group, 1992.

Edwards, Paul and Sarah. *Working From Home: Everything You Need to Know about Living and Working under the Same Roof*. New York: G. P. Putnam's Sons, 1994.

Levinson, Jay Conrad. *Guerilla Marketing: How to Make Big Profits from Your Small Business*. Boston: Houghton Mifflin Co., 1985.

Parker, Lucy V. *How to Open and Operate a Home-Based Writing Business*. Old Saybrook, Conn.: Globe Pequot Press, 1994.

### Periodicals

Note: Subscription prices are approximate as of January 1995.

*Communication Arts Magazine*. Subscription Department, P.O. Box 10300, Palo Alto, CA 94303–9979. Four issues plus four supplements each year, $50. Respected voice of the

American graphic-design industry, with emphasis on electronic publishing.

*Entrepreneur.* Subscription Department, P.O. Box 50368, Boulder, CO 80321–0368. Monthly, $20 per year.

*Home Office Computing.* P.O. Box 51344, Boulder, CO 80321–1344. Monthly. For subscription information, call (800) 288–7812.

*The Working Communicator.* Ragan Communications, 212 W. Superior, Suite 200, Chicago, IL 60610. Monthly eight-page newsletter plus four books, $89. Published primarily for corporate communications professionals, with new ideas, trends, and techniques.

# Selected Resources

## On-Line Services

**America Online**
8619 Westwood Center Drive
Vienna, VA 22182–2285
(800) 827–6364

**CompuServe**
P.O. Box 20212
Columbus, OH 43320
(800) 368–3343

**Prodigy**
445 Hamilton Avenue
White Plains, NY 10601
(800) 776–3449

## Copyright Information

**United States Copyright Office**
Library of Congress
Washington, DC 20559
Information line:
(202) 707–3000 (ask for information packet 118)

## Trademark Registration

**U.S. Patent and Trademark Office,**
Washington, DC 20231
(703) 308–HELP

## U.S. Government–Sponsored Business Assistance

**Service Corps of Retired Executives (SCORE)**
409 Third Street SW,
   Suite 5900
Washington, DC 20476
(202) 205-6759

**Small Business Administration**
409 Third Street SW
Washington, DC 20476
(800) U-ASK-SBA
Personnel locator:
   (202) 205-6600

## Tax Information

*Business Use of Your Home*
IRS Publication 587
Call (800) TAX-FORM

## National Organizations

**American Home Business Association**
P.O. Box 995
Darien, CT 06820-0995
(203) 655-4380

**International Association of Business Communicators (IABC)**
One Hallidie Plaza, Suite 600
San Francisco, CA 94102
(415) 433-3400
fax (415) 362-8762

**Mother's Home Business Network**
P. O. Box 423
East Meadow, NY 11554
(516) 997-7394

**National Association for the Cottage Industry**
P.O. Box 14850
Chicago, IL 60614
(312) 472-8116

**National Association for the Self Employed (NASE)**
Information Services
PO Box 869023
Plano, TX 75086-9899

**National Association of Home-Based Businesses**
P.O. Box 30220
Baltimore, MD 21270
(410) 363-3698

**National Association of Women Business Owners**
600 S. Federal Street,
   Suite 400
Chicago, IL 60605
(312) 922-0465

**Public Relations Society of America (PRSA)**
National Office:
33 Irving Place, 3rd Floor
New York, NY 10003–2376
(212) 995–2230
fax: (212) 995–0797

**Society for Technical Communication**
901 Stuart Street
Arlington, VA 22203
(703) 522–4114

**Women in Communications, Inc.**
2101 Wilson Boulevard, Suite 417
Arlington, VA 22201
(703) 528–4200
fax (703) 528–4205

# Networking Organizations

**The Network**
(800) 825–8286 or
(909) 624–2227

**Leads Club**
(800) 783–3761 or
(619) 434–3761

**LeTip**
(800) 255–3847 or
(619) 275–0600

# Other

Paper Direct, a direct-mail supplier of formats, supplies, and software for laser-printed marketing materials. For catalog, call (800) A–PAPERS.

# INDEX

# About the Author

Louann Werksma's twenty years of in-depth experience in writing, editing, marketing, public relations, and corporate communications are evident in the quality publications produced by the communications company she founded in 1986, Wordwerks Communications. Today, Wordwerks' clients include healthcare institutions, educational publishers, and corporations of all sizes.

Ms. Werksma combines a corporate sales and marketing background with a communications degree and experience in advertising, reporting, feature writing, and book editing. Prior to founding Wordwerks, she served as the public relations coordinator for a PBS affiliate television station, a news reporter for a metropolitan daily newspaper, a magazine editor, and director of educational services for a Connecticut textbook publishing company.

As a freelance editor, she has been hired by major publishers to ghostwrite for well-known authors. *How to Open and Operate a Home-Based Communications Business* is the first book she has written that bears her name.

Ms. Werksma operates Wordwerks Communications from her home in Grand Haven, Michigan, where she lives with her husband, Henry, a marketing executive, and their sons Jared, Matthew, and Patrick.